SHAMBHALA LIBRARY

Writing Down the Bones

*Expanded edition with a preface
and interview with the author*

Natalie Goldberg

Shambhala
Boston & London
2010

FRONTISPIECE: *Gini's Kitchen*, 1992, ink and gouache, by
Natalie Goldberg.

Shambhala Publications, Inc.
Horticultural Hall
300 Massachusetts Avenue
Boston, Massachusetts 02115
www.shambhala.com

9 8 7 6 5 4 3

PRINTED IN CHINA

⊗This edition is printed on acid-free paper that meets the
American National Standards Institute z39.48 Standard.
♻Shambhala Publications makes every effort to print on recycled paper.
For more information please visit www.shambhala.com.
Distributed in the United States by Random House, Inc.,
and in Canada by Random House of Canada Ltd

Page 240 constitutes a continuation of the copyright page.

*The Library of Congress catalogues the trade paperback edition
of this book as follows:*
Goldberg, Natalie.
Writing down the bones.
1. Authorship. I. Title.
PN145.C64 1986 808'.02 86-11840
ISBN 978-0-87773-375-1 (pbk.)
ISBN 978-1-57062-258-8 (cloth)
ISBN 978-1-59030-316-0 (Shambhala Pocket Classics)
ISBN 978-1-59030-261-3 (revised pbk. edition)
ISBN 978-1-59030-794-6 (Shambhala Library)

For all my students
past, present, and future

May we all meet in heaven café
writing for eternity.

CONTENTS

Contents

PREFACE

A YEAR AGO on a December night in Santa Fe, New Mexico, I attended the birthday party of a young filmmaker I had known only briefly. For about half an hour I stood near the buffet table in conversation with a man in his early thirties, who I had just met. He was obviously a serious poet; I told him I was once a poet, too, before I'd written my first book. We bantered back and forth. I was enjoying myself immensely.

Suddenly, with a quizzical look on his face, he asked, "So, anyway, what have you written?"

"Well, several books," I said, "but the one I'm most known for is called *Writing Down the Bones.*"

"You're kidding!" His eyes bugged out. "I thought you were dead."

Without blinking an eye, I responded, "No, not yet. Still trucking along, still putting pen to paper."

We both laughed.

He didn't need to say any more. I understood: he'd read me in high school. All books read then must be by deceased men—or women. No author studied in a secondary school institution could possibly be alive.

Writing Down the Bones came out in 1986. I have

often told audiences that if it had been published in the fifties it would have flopped. But instead it met this country exactly where it was—great hordes of Americans had a need to express themselves. Writing is egalitarian; it cuts across geographic, class, gender, and racial lines. I received fan letters from vice presidents of insurance agencies in Florida; factory workers in Nebraska; quarry workers in Missouri; prisoners in Texas; lawyers, doctors, gay rights activists, housewives, librarians, teachers, priests, politicians. A whole revolution in writing began soon after it came out. Separate writing sections in bookstores sprang up. One student said to me, "I get it! Writing is the new religion."

"But why," people asked me, "does everybody want to write?"

I don't think everyone wants to create the great American novel, but we all have a dream of telling our stories—of realizing what we think, feel, and see before we die. Writing is a path to meet ourselves and become intimate. Think about it: Ants don't do it. Trees don't. Not even thoroughbred horses, mountain elk, house cats, grass, or rocks do it. Writing is a uniquely human activity. It might even be built into our DNA. It should be put forward in the Declaration of Independence, along with the other inalienable rights: "Life, liberty, and the pursuit of happiness—and writing."

And it's inexpensive. All you need is pen, paper (of

course, computer, if you are so inclined), and the human mind. What crannies of untouched perception can you explore? What autumn was it that the moon entered your life? When was it that you picked blueberries at their quintessential moment? How long did you wait for your first true bike? Who are your angels? What are you thinking of? Not thinking of? What are you looking at? Not looking at? Writing can give you confidence, can train you to wake up.

Writing Down the Bones is backed by a two-thousand-year-old practice of studying the mind. It is not solely Natalie's creative idea. I wanted to root this work, give it a solid foundation. At the time I wrote it, I had already studied meditation for ten years, six in close practice with a Japanese Zen master. Where do thoughts come from? Memories, ideas, even the word *the*? Meditation and writing practice are coincident. The more we understand the human mind, our basic writing tool, the better, more secure we can be in our writing.

When this book came out, people called me a genius. I smiled, but I knew I wasn't a genius. Maybe the only genius moment was having Zen inform the writing. I had a sincere and earnest desire to figure out this writing life. I very badly wanted to do it and I didn't know how, and I hadn't learned how in all my public school education. By college, I think I gave up. But I had a yearning for it way deep underneath, a desire I didn't even know I had. I was in love with reading and literature. There were stories only I knew about my family, about my first kiss, last haircut, the smell of sage on a mesa and my kinship with the flat plains of Nebraska. I had to get slow and dumb (not take anything for granted) and watch and see how everything connects, how you contact your thoughts and lay them down on paper.

I wish now that I had another chance to write that school composition, "What I Did Last Summer." When I wrote it in fifth grade, I was scared and just recorded: "It was interesting. It was nice. My summer was fun." I snuck through with a B grade. But I still wondered, How do you really do that? Now it is obvious. You tell the truth and you depict it in detail: My mother dyed her hair red and polished her toenails silver. I was mad for Parcheesi and running in the sprinkler, catching beetles in a mason jar and feeding them grass. My father sat at the kitchen table a lot staring straight ahead, never talking, a Budweiser in his hand.

What an opportunity to recount the crush I had on a blond boy down the block, the news of racial injustice I saw on TV and how I felt confused and hurt by it, how I feared my sister was prettier than me, how I made coleslaw with my grandma. But I didn't know how to narrate all these things.

In this book, I instruct all of us how—the old students, and the young.

It is my sincere wish that this book be taught in all public and private schools, that students learn how to do writing practice, that they come to know themselves, feel joy in expression, trust what they think. Once you connect with your mind, you are who you are and you're free.

A long time ago I read Jack Kerouac's essentials for prose. Four of them, in particular, have provided me with heart for the path:

Accept loss forever
Be submissive to everything, open, listening
No fear or shame in the dignity of your experience,
    language, and knowledge
Be in love with your life

Believe me, you, too, can find your place inside the huge terrain of writing. No one is so odd as to be left out.

Now, please, go. Write your asses off.

—DECEMBER 2004

Introduction

I was a Goody Two-Shoes all through school. I wanted my teachers to like me. I learned commas, colons, semicolons. I wrote compositions with clear sentences that were dull and boring. Nowhere was there an original thought or genuine feeling. I was eager to give the teachers what I thought they wanted.

In college I was in love with literature. I mean wild about it. I typed poems by Gerard Manley Hopkins over and over again so I could memorize them. I read John Milton, Shelley, Keats aloud and then swooned on my narrow bed in the dormitory. In college in the late sixties, I read almost exclusively male writers, usually dead, from England and the rest of Europe. They were very far removed from my daily life, and though I loved them, none of them reflected my experience. I must have subconsciously surmised that writing was not within my ken. It never occurred to me to write, though I secretly wanted to marry a poet.

After I graduated college and discovered that no one was going to hire me to read novels and swoon over poetry, three friends and I started a co-op restaurant and cooked and served natural food lunches in the basement of the Newman Center in Ann

Arbor, Michigan. This was the early seventies, and one year before the opening of the restaurant I had tasted my first avocado. The restaurant was called Naked Lunch, after the novel by William Burroughs—"a frozen moment when everyone sees what is on the end of every fork." In the morning I baked muffins with raisins and muffins with blueberries or even with peanut butter if I wanted. Naturally, I hoped the customers would like them, but I knew if I cared about the muffins, they usually were good. We had created the restaurant. There was no great answer outside ourselves that would get us an A in school anymore. It was the very beginning of learning to trust my own mind.

One Tuesday I was making ratatouille for lunch. When you make it for a restaurant, you don't cut up one onion and one eggplant. The counter was filled with onions, eggplants, zucchinis, tomatoes, and garlic. I spent several hours chopping and slicing. Walking home from work that night, I stopped in the Centicore Bookstore on State Street and wandered up and down the aisles. I saw a thin volume of poetry entitled *Fruits and Vegetables* by Erica Jong. (Jong had not come out with her novel *Fear of Flying* yet and was still unknown.) The first poem I opened to in the book was about cooking an eggplant! I was amazed: "You mean you can write about something like that?" Something as ordinary as that? Something that I did in my life? A synapse connected in my brain. I went home with the resolve to write what I knew and to trust my own thoughts and feelings and to not look outside myself. I was not in school anymore: I could say what I wanted. I began to write about my family because nobody could say I was wrong. I knew them better than anyone else.

This all happened fifteen years ago. A friend once told me: "Trust in love and it will take you where you need to go." I want to add, "Trust in *what* you love, continue to do it, and it will take you where you need to go." And don't worry too much about security. You will eventually have a deep security when you begin to do what you want. How many of us with our big salaries are actually secure anyway?

I have taught writing workshops for the last eleven years at the University of New Mexico; at the Lama Foundation; to the hippies in Taos, New Mexico; for nuns in Albuquerque; to juvenile delinquents in Boulder; at the University of Minnesota; at Northeast College, a technical school in Norfolk, Nebraska; as Minnesota Poet-in-the-Schools; at Sunday-night writing groups in my home, to gay men's groups. I teach the same methods over and over again. It is such basic information about trusting your own mind and creating a confidence in your experience that I have never grown tired of teaching it. Instead my understanding continues to deepen.

In 1974 I began to do sitting meditation. From 1978 to 1984 I studied Zen formally with Dainin Katagiri

Roshi (*Roshi* is a title for a Zen master) at the Minnesota Zen Center in Minneapolis. Whenever I went to see him and asked him a question about Buddhism, I had trouble understanding the answer until he said, "You know, like in writing when you . . ." When he referred to writing, I understood. About three years ago he said to me, "Why do you come to sit meditation? Why don't you make writing your practice? If you go deep enough in writing, it will take you everyplace."

This book is about writing. It is also about using writing as your practice, as a way to help you penetrate your life and become sane. What is said here about writing can be applied to running, painting, anything you love and have chosen to work with in your life. When I read several chapters to my friend John Rollwagen, president of Cray Research, he said, "Why, Natalie, you're talking about business. That's the way it is in business. There is no difference."

Learning to write is not a linear process. There is no logical A-to-B-to-C way to become a good writer. One neat truth about writing cannot answer it all. There are many truths. To do writing practice means to deal ultimately with your whole life. If you receive instructions on how to set a broken bone in your ankle, you can't use those same instructions to fill a cavity in your teeth. You might read a section in this book that says to be very specific and precise. That's to help the ailment of abstract, general meandering in your writing. But then you read another chapter that says lose control, write on waves of emotion. That's to encourage you to really say deep down what you need to say. Or in one chapter it says to fix up a studio, that you need a private place to write; the next chapter says, "Get out of the house, away from the dirty dishes. Go write in a café." Some techniques are appropriate at some times and some for other times. Every moment is different. Different things work. One isn't wrong and the other right.

When I teach a class, I want the students to be "writing down the bones," the essential, awake speech of their minds. But I also know I can't just say, "Okay, write clearly and with great honesty." In class we try different techniques or methods. Eventually, the students hit the mark, come home to what they need to say and how they need to say it. But it is rarely, "Okay, in the third class after we have covered this and this, you will write well."

It is the same for reading this book. The book can be read consecutively and that may be good the first time through. You may also open to any chapter and read it. Each chapter is designed to be its own whole. Relax as you read and absorb it, as by osmosis, with your whole body and mind. And don't just read it. Write. Trust yourself. Learn your own needs. Use this book.

Beginner's Mind, Pen and Paper

When I teach a beginning class, it is good. I have to come back to beginner's mind, the first way I thought and felt about writing. In a sense, that beginner's mind is what we must come back to every time we sit down and write. There is no security, no assurance that because we wrote something good two months ago, we will do it again. Actually, every time we begin, we wonder how we ever did it before. Each time is a new journey with no maps.

So when I teach a writing group, I have to tell the story all over again and remember that the students are hearing it for the first time. I must begin at the very beginning.

First, consider the pen you write with. It should be a fast-writing pen because your thoughts are always much faster than your hand. You don't want to slow up your hand even more with a slow pen. A ballpoint, a pencil, a felt tip, for sure, are slow. Go to a stationery store and see what feels good to you. Try out different kinds. Don't get too fancy and expensive. I mostly use a cheap Sheaffer fountain pen, about $1.95. It has replaceable cartridges. I've bought hundreds over the years. I've had every color; they often leak, but they are fast. The new roller pens that are out now are fast too, but there's a slight loss of control. You want to be able to feel the connection and texture of the pen on paper.

Think, too, about your notebook. It is important. This is your equipment, like hammer and nails to a carpenter. (Feel fortunate—for very little money you are in business!) Sometimes people buy expensive hardcover journals. They are bulky and heavy, and because they are fancy, you are compelled to write something good. Instead you should feel that you have permission to write the worst junk in the world and it would be okay. Give yourself a lot of space in which to explore writing. A cheap spiral notebook lets you feel that you can fill it quickly and afford another. Also, it is easy to carry. (I often buy notebook-size purses.)

Garfield, the Muppets, Mickey Mouse, Star Wars. I use notebooks with funny covers. They come out fresh in September when school starts. They are a quarter more than the plain spirals, but I like them. I can't take myself too seriously when I open up a Peanuts notebook. It also helps me locate them more easily—"Oh, yes, that summer I wrote in the rodeo series notebooks." Try out different kinds—blank, lined, or graphed pages, hard or soft-covered. In the end, it must work for you.

The size of your notebook matters too. A small notebook can be kept in your pocket, but then you have small thoughts. That's okay. William Carlos

Williams, the famous American poet who was also a children's doctor, wrote many of his poems on prescription pads in between office visits by his patients.

Detail

Doc, I bin lookin' for you
I owe you two bucks.

How you doin'?

Fine. When I get it
I'll bring it up to you.[1]

You can find many prescription-pad-size poems in his collected works.

Sometimes, instead of writing in a notebook, you might want to directly type out your thoughts. Writing is physical and is affected by the equipment you use. In typing, your fingers hit keys and the result is block, black letters: a different aspect of yourself may come out. I have found that when I am writing something emotional, I must write it the first time directly with hand on paper. Handwriting is more connected to the movement of the heart. Yet, when I tell stories, I go straight to the typewriter.

Another thing you can try is speaking into a tape recorder and feeling how it is to directly record your voice speaking your thoughts. Or you might use it for convenience' sake: you might be working on the hem of a dress and you begin to think how it was with your ex-husband and you want to write about it. Your hands are busy sewing; you can talk about it into a recorder.

I have not worked very much with a computer, but I can imagine using a Macintosh, where the keyboard can be put on my lap, closing my eyes and just typing away. The computer automatically returns the carriage. The device is called "wraparound." You can rap nonstop. You don't have to worry about the typewriter ringing a little bell at the end of a line.

Experiment. Even try writing in a big drawing pad. It is true that the inside world creates the outside world, but the outside world and our tools also affect the way we form our thoughts. Try skywriting.

Choose your tools carefully, but not so carefully that you get uptight or spend more time at the stationery store than at your writing table.

First Thoughts

THE BASIC UNIT of writing practice is the timed exercise. You may time yourself for ten minutes, twenty minutes, or an hour. It's up to you. At the beginning you may want to start small and after a week increase your time, or you may want to dive in for an hour the first time. It doesn't matter. What does matter is that whatever amount of time you choose for that session, you must commit yourself to it and for that full period:

1. *Keep your hand moving.* (Don't pause to reread the line you have just written. That's stalling and trying to get control of what you're saying.)
2. *Don't cross out.* (That is editing as you write. Even if you write something you didn't mean to write, leave it.)
3. *Don't worry about spelling, punctuation, grammar.* (Don't even care about staying within the margins and lines on the page.)
4. *Lose control.*
5. *Don't think. Don't get logical.*
6. *Go for the jugular.* (If something comes up in

your writing that is scary or naked, dive right into it. It probably has lots of energy.)

These are the rules. It is important to adhere to them because the aim is to burn through to first thoughts, to the place where energy is unobstructed by social politeness or the internal censor, to the place where you are writing what your mind actually sees and feels, not what it thinks it should see or feel. It's a great opportunity to capture the oddities of your mind. Explore the rugged edge of thought. Like grating a carrot, give the paper the colorful coleslaw of your consciousness.

First thoughts have tremendous energy. It is the way the mind first flashes on something. The internal censor usually squelches them, so we live in the realm of second and third thoughts, thoughts on thought, twice and three times removed from the direct connection of the first fresh flash. For instance, the phrase "I cut the daisy from my throat" shot through my mind. Now my second thought, carefully tutored in $1 + 1 = 2$ logic, in politeness, fear, and embarrassment at the natural, would say, "That's ridiculous. You sound suicidal. Don't show yourself cutting your throat. Someone will think you are crazy." And instead, if we give the censor its way, we write, "My throat was a little sore, so I didn't say anything." Proper and boring.

First thoughts are also unencumbered by ego, by that mechanism in us that tries to be in control, tries to prove the world is permanent and solid, enduring and logical. The world is not permanent, is ever-changing and full of human suffering. So if you express something egoless, it is also full of energy because it is expressing the truth of the way things are. You are not carrying the burden of ego in your expression, but are riding for moments the waves of human consciousness and using your personal details to express the ride.

In Zen meditation you sit on a cushion called a zafu with your legs crossed, back straight, hands at your knees or in front of you in a gesture called a mudra. You face a white wall and watch your breath. No matter what you feel—great tornadoes of anger and resistance, thunderstorms of joy and grief—you continue to sit, back straight, legs crossed, facing the wall. You learn to not be tossed away no matter how great the thought or emotion. That is the discipline: to continue to sit.

The same is true in writing. You must be a great warrior when you contact first thoughts and write from them. Especially at the beginning you may feel great emotions and energy that will sweep you away, but you don't stop writing. You continue to use your pen and record the details of your life and penetrate into the heart of them. Often in a beginning class students break down crying when they read pieces they have written. That is okay. Often as they write they cry, too. However, I encourage them to continue reading or writing right through the tears so they may come out the other side and not be thrown off by the emotion. Don't stop at the tears; go through to truth. This is the discipline.

Why else are first thoughts so energizing? Because they have to do with freshness and inspiration. Inspiration means "breathing in." Breathing in God. You actually become larger than yourself, and first thoughts are present. They are not a cover-up of what is actually happening or being felt. The present is imbued with tremendous energy. It is what is. My friend who is a Buddhist said once after coming out of a meditation retreat, "The colors were so much more vibrant afterward." Her meditation teacher said, "When you are present, the world is truly alive."

Writing as a Practice

THIS IS THE PRACTICE school of writing. Like running, the more you do it, the better you get at it. Some days you don't want to run and you resist every step of the three miles, but you do it anyway. You practice whether you want to or not. You don't wait around for inspiration and a deep desire to run. It'll never happen, especially if you are out of shape and have been avoiding it. But if you run regularly, you train your mind to cut through or ignore your resistance. You just do it. And in the middle of the run, you love it. When you come to the end, you never want to stop. And you stop, hungry for the next time.

That's how writing is, too. Once you're deep into it, you wonder what took you so long to finally settle down at the desk. Through practice you actually do get better. You learn to trust your deep self more and not give in to your voice that wants to avoid writing. It is odd that we never question the feasibility of a football team practicing long hours for one game; yet in writing we rarely give ourselves the space for practice.

When you write, don't say, "I'm going to write a poem." That attitude will freeze you right away. Sit down with the least expectation of yourself; say, "I am free to write the worst junk in the world." You have to give yourself the space to write a lot without a destination. I've had students who said they decided they were going to write the great American novel and haven't written a line since. If every time you sat down, you expected something great, writing would always be a great disappointment. Plus that expectation would also keep you from writing.

My rule is to finish a notebook a month. (I'm always making up writing guidelines for myself.) Simply to fill it. That is the practice. My ideal is to write every day. I say it is my ideal. I am careful not to pass judgment or create anxiety if I don't do that. No one lives up to his ideal.

In my notebooks I don't bother with the side margin or the one at the top: I fill the whole page. I am not writing anymore for a teacher or for school. I am writing for myself first and I don't have to stay within my limits, not even margins. This gives me a psychological freedom and permission. And when my writing is on and I'm really cooking, I usually forget about punctuation, spelling, etc. I also notice that my handwriting changes. It becomes larger and looser.

Often I can look around the room at my students as they write and can tell which ones are really on and present at a given time in their writing. They are more intensely involved and their bodies are hanging loose. Again, it is like running. There's little resistance when the run is good. All of you is moving; there's no you separate from the runner. In writing, when you are truly on, there's no writer, no paper, no pen, no thoughts. Only writing does writing—everything else is gone.

One of the main aims in writing practice is to learn to trust your own mind and body; to grow patient and nonaggressive. Art lives in the Big World. One poem or story doesn't matter one way or the other. It's the process of writing and life that matters. Too many writers have written great books and gone insane or alcoholic or killed themselves. This process teaches about sanity. We are trying to become sane along with our poems and stories.

Chögyam Trungpa, Rinpoche, a Tibetan Buddhist master, said, "We must continue to open in the face of tremendous opposition. No one is encouraging us to open and still we must peel away the layers of the heart." It is the same with this way of practice writing: We must continue to open and trust in our own voice and process. Ultimately, if the process is good, the end will be good. You will get good writing.

A friend once said that when she had a good black-and-white drawing that she was going to add color to, she always practiced first on a few drawings she didn't care about in order to warm up. This writing practice is also a warm-up for anything else you might want to write. It is the bottom line, the most primitive, essential beginning of writing. The trust you learn in your own voice can be directed then into a business letter, a novel, a Ph.D. dissertation, a play, a memoir. But it is something you must come back to again and again. Don't think, "I got it! I know how to write. I trust my voice. I'm off to write the great American novel." It's good to go off and write a novel, but don't stop doing writing practice. It is what keeps you in tune, like a dancer who does warm-ups before dancing or a runner who does stretches before running. Runners don't say, "Oh, I ran yesterday. I'm limber." Each day they warm up and stretch.

Writing practice embraces your whole life and doesn't demand any logical form: no chapter 19 following the action in chapter 18. It's a place that you can come to wild and unbridled, mixing the dream of your grandmother's soup with the astounding clouds outside your window. It is undirected and has to do with all of you right in your present moment. Think of writing practice as loving arms you come to illogically and incoherently. It's our wild forest where we gather energy before going to prune our garden, write our fine books and novels. It's a continual practice.

Sit down right now. Give me this moment. Write whatever's running through you. You might start with "this moment" and end up writing about the gardenia you wore at your wedding seven years ago. That's fine. Don't try to control it. Stay present with whatever comes up, and keep your hand moving.

Composting

IT TAKES A WHILE for our experience to sift through our consciousness. For instance, it is hard to write about being in love in the midst of a mad love affair. We have no perspective. All we can say is, "I'm madly in love," over and over again. It is also hard to write about a city we just moved to; it's not yet in our body. We don't know our new home, even if we can drive to the drugstore without getting lost. We have not lived through three winters there or seen the ducks leave in fall and return to the lakes in spring. Hemingway wrote about Michigan while sitting in a café in Paris. "Maybe away from Paris I could write about Paris as in Paris I could write about Michigan. I did not know it was too early for that because I did not know Paris well enough."[2]

Our senses by themselves are dumb. They take in experience, but they need the richness of sifting for a while through our consciousness and through our whole bodies. I call this "composting." Our bodies are garbage heaps: we collect experience, and from the decomposition of the thrown-out eggshells, spinach leaves, coffee grinds, and old steak bones of our minds come nitrogen, heat, and very fertile soil. Out of this fertile soil bloom our poems and stories. But this does not come all at once. It takes time. Continue to turn over and over the organic details of your life until some of them fall through the garbage of discursive thoughts to the solid ground of black soil.

When I have students who have written many pages and read them in class, and the writing is not all necessarily good but I see that they are exploring their minds for material, I am glad. I know those people will continue and are not just obsessed with "hot" writing, but are in the process of practice. They are raking their minds and taking their shallow thinking and turning it over. If we continue to work with this raw matter, it will draw us deeper and deeper into ourselves, but not in a neurotic way. We will begin to see the rich garden we have inside us and use that for writing.

Often I will stab many times at something I want to say. For instance, you can look in my notebooks from August through December 1983 and see that I attempted several times a month to write about my father dying. I was exploring and composting the material. Then suddenly, and I can't say how, in December I sat transfixed at the Croissant Express in Minneapolis and a long poem about that subject poured out of me. All the disparate things I had to say were suddenly fused with energy and unity—a bright red tulip shot out of the compost. Katagiri Roshi said: "Your little will can't do anything. It takes Great

Determination. Great Determination doesn't mean just you making an effort. It means the whole universe is behind you and with you—the birds, trees, sky, moon, and ten directions." Suddenly, after much composting, you are in alignment with the stars or the moment or the dining-room chandelier above your head, and your body opens and speaks.

Understanding this process cultivates patience and produces less anxiety. We aren't running everything, not even the writing we do. At the same time, we must keep practicing. It is not an excuse to not write and sit on the couch eating bonbons. We must continue to work the compost pile, enriching it and making it fertile so that something beautiful may bloom and so that our writing muscles are in good shape to ride the universe when it moves through us.

This understanding also helps us to accept someone else's success and not to be too greedy. It is simply that person's time. Ours will come in this lifetime or the next. No matter. Continue to practice.

Artistic Stability

I HAVE A PILE OF spiral notebooks about five feet high that begin around 1977, my early years of writing in Taos, New Mexico. I want to throw them out—who can bear to look at the junk of our own minds that comes out in writing practice? I have a friend in New Mexico who makes solar houses out of beer cans and old tires. I think I will try to build one out of discarded spiral notebooks. A friend who lives upstairs says, "Don't get rid of them." I tell her she can have them if she wants.

I pile them on her stairs leading up to her apartment and leave for Norfolk, Nebraska, for four days to do a writing workshop. When I return she looks at me oddly, plunks herself down in the old pink chair in my bedroom: "I've been reading your notebooks all weekend. They are so intimate; so scared, insecure for pages, then suddenly they are not you—just raw energy and wild mind. And now here you are—Natalie—in the flesh, just a person. It feels so funny." I feel good because I don't care that she sees how I really am. I'm glad. I want someone to know me. We walk through so many myths of each other and ourselves;

we are so thankful when someone sees us for who we are and accepts us.

She said it was empowering to read my notebooks because she realized that I really did write "shit," sometimes for whole notebooks. Often I tell my students, "Listen, I write and still write terrible self-pitying stuff for page after page." They don't believe me. Reading my notebooks is living proof of that. My upstairs neighbor said, "If you could write the junk you did then and write the stuff you do now, I realize I can do anything. There's so much power in the mind. I feel like who knows what I can do!" She said the main thing she saw in the notebooks—whole notebooks of complaints, boring description, and flagrant anger—was an absolute trust in the process. "I saw that you kept on writing even when you wrote, 'I must be nuts to do this.'"

It is true that I believed in the process. I was living in the boredom of long, dry days in the hills of New Mexico, where *Jaws* played for six consecutive months in the only movie theater in Taos. I had a belief in something real below the surface of life or right in the middle of life, but often my own mind kept me asleep or diverted; yet my own mind and life were also all I had. So I began writing out of them. "I see as I progress through the notebooks that this kind of writing gave you who you are. It's a verification of being human."

When you begin to write this way—right out of

your own mind—you might have to be willing to write junk for five years, because we have accumulated it over many more than that and have been gladly avoiding it in ourselves. We have to look at our own inertia, insecurities, self-hate, fear that, in truth, we have nothing valuable to say. It is true that when we begin anything new, resistances fly in our face. Now you have the opportunity to not run or be tossed away, but to look at them black and white on paper and see what their silly voices say. When your writing blooms out of the back of this garbage and compost, it is very stable. You are not running from anything. You can have a sense of artistic security. If you are not afraid of the voices inside you, you will not fear the critics outside you. Besides, those voices are merely guardians and demons protecting the real treasure, the first thoughts of the mind.

Actually, when I look at my old notebooks, I think I have been a bit self-indulgent and have given myself too much time to meander in my discursive thoughts. I could have cut through sooner. Yet it is good to know about our terrible selves, not laud or criticize them, just acknowledge them. Then, out of this knowledge, we are better equipped to make a choice for beauty, kind consideration, and clear truth. We make this choice with our feet firmly on the ground. We are not running wildly after beauty with fear at our backs.

A List of Topics for Writing Practice

S OMETIMES WE SIT down to write and can't think of anything to write about. The blank page can be intimidating, and it does get boring to write over and over again for ten minutes of practice, "I can't think of what to say. I can't think of what to say." It is a good idea to have a page in your notebook where you jot down, as they come to you, ideas of topics to write about. It could be a line you heard. For example, at a restaurant I complained to one waiter about another one. His response: "I know he's odd, but if they dance to a different drummer I say, 'Just let them dance.'" It could be a flash of memory: your grandfather's false teeth; how the lilacs smelled last June when you weren't there; who you were in your saddle shoes at eight years old. It could be anything. Add to the list anytime you think of something. Then when you sit down to write, you can just grab a topic from that list and begin.

Making a list is good. It makes you start noticing material for writing in your daily life, and your writing comes out of a relationship with your life and its texture. In this way, the composting process is beginning. Your body is starting to digest and turn over your material, so even when you are not actually at the desk physically writing, there are parts of you raking, fertilizing, taking in the sun's heat, and making ready for the deep green plants of writing to grow.

If you give your mind too much time to contemplate a beginning when you sit down to write, your monkey mind might meander over many topics and never quite get to putting a word on the page. So the list also helps to activate your writing quickly and cut through resistance. Naturally, once you begin writing you might be surprised where your mind takes the topic. That's good. You are not trying to control your writing. You are stepping out of the way. Keep your hand moving.

But until you get your own list, here are some writing ideas:

1. Tell about the quality of light coming in through your window. Jump in and write. Don't worry if it is night and your curtains are closed or you would rather write about the light up north—just write. Go for ten minutes, fifteen, a half hour.

2. Begin with "I remember." Write lots of small memories. If you fall into one large memory, write that. Just keep going. Don't be concerned if the memory happened five seconds ago or five years ago. Everything that isn't this moment is memory coming alive again as you write. If you

get stuck, just repeat the phrase "I remember" again and keep going.

3. Take something you feel strongly about, whether it is positive or negative, and write about it as though you love it. Go as far as you can, writing as though you love it, then flip over and write about the same thing as though you hate it. Then write about it perfectly neutral.

4. Choose a color—for instance, pink—and take a fifteen-minute walk. On your walk notice wherever there is pink. Come back to your notebook and write for fifteen minutes.

5. Write in different places—for example, in a laundromat, and pick up on the rhythm of the washing machines. Write at bus stops, in cafés. Write what is going on around you.

6. Give me your morning. Breakfast, waking up, walking to the bus stop. Be as specific as possible. Slow down in your mind and go over the details of the morning.

7. Visualize a place that you really love, be there, see the details. Now write about it. It could be a corner of your bedroom, an old tree you sat under one whole summer, a table at McDonald's in your neighborhood, a place by a river. What colors are there, sounds, smells? When someone else reads it, she should know what it is like to be there. She should feel how you love

it, not by your saying you love it, but by your handling of the details.

8. Write about "leaving." Approach it any way you want. Write about your divorce, leaving the house this morning, or a friend dying.

9. What is your first memory?

10. Who are the people you have loved?

11. Write about the streets of your city.

12. Describe a grandparent.

13. Write about:

> swimming
> the stars
> the most frightened you've ever been
> green places
> how you learned about sex
> your first sexual experience
> the closest you ever felt to God or nature
> reading and books that have changed your life
> physical endurance
> a teacher you had

Don't be abstract. Write the real stuff. Be honest and detailed.

14. Take a poetry book. Open to any page, grab a line, write it down, and continue from there. A friend calls it "writing off the page." If you begin with a great line, it helps because you start right off from a lofty place. "I will die in Paris, on a

rainy day. . . . It will be a Thursday," by the poet Cesar Vallejo.[3] "I will die on Monday at eleven o'clock, on Friday at three o'clock in South Dakota riding a tractor, in Brooklyn in a delicatessen," on and on. Every time you get stuck, just rewrite your first line and keep going. Rewriting the first line gives you a whole new start and a chance for another direction—"I don't want to die and I don't care if I'm in Paris or Moscow or Youngstown, Ohio."

15. What kind of animal are you? Do you think you are really a cow, chipmunk, fox, horse underneath?

Start to generate your own writing material and topics. It is good practice.

Fighting Tofu

DISCIPLINE has always been a cruel word. I always think of it as beating my lazy part into submission, and that never works. The dictator and the resister continue to fight:

"I don't want to write."

"You are going to write."

"I'll write later. I'm tired."

"You'll write now."

All the while my notebook remains empty. It's another way that ego has to continue to struggle. Katagiri Roshi has a wonderful term: "fighting the tofu." Tofu is cheese made out of soybeans. It is dense, bland, white. It is fruitless to wrestle with it; you get nowhere.

If those characters in you want to fight, let them fight. Meanwhile, the sane part of you should quietly get up, go over to your notebook, and begin to write from a deeper, more peaceful place. Unfortunately, those two fighters often come with you to your notebook since they are inside your head. We can't always leave them in the backyard or basement or at the day-care center. So you might have to give them five or ten minutes of voice in your notebook. Let them carry on in writing. It is amazing that when you give those voices writing space, their complaining quickly gets boring and you get sick of them.

It's just resistance. Ego can be very creative and make up remarkable resistive tactics. My friend who was beginning her first novel said that she would sit at the typewriter for the first ten minutes and just write about what a terrible writer she was, what a jerk she was to even attempt a novel. Then she pulled out that sheet of paper, tore it up, and began on the task at hand—the next chapter of her novel.

It is important to have a way worked out to begin your writing; otherwise, washing the dishes becomes the most important thing on earth—anything that will divert you from writing. Finally, one just has to shut up, sit down, and write. That is painful. Writing is so simple, basic, and austere. There are no fancy gadgets to make it more attractive. Our monkey minds would much rather discuss our resistances with a friend at a lovely restaurant or go to a therapist to work out our writing blocks. We like to complicate simple tasks. There is a Zen saying: "Talk when you talk, walk when you walk, and die when you die." Write when you write. Stop battling yourself with guilt, accusations, and strong-arm threats.

But after saying all this, I will tell you a few tricks I have done in the past to nudge me along:

1. I haven't written anything in a while. I call a writing friend and make a date with her to meet in a week and go over our work. I have to write something to show her.

2. I teach writing groups and have to do the assignments I give the class. I didn't wait for years of writing before I began to teach writing. I was living in Taos, and there were few writers there ten years ago. I needed writing friends, so I began a women's writing group. In teaching them, I learned to write. Baba Hari Dass, an Indian yogi, says: "Teach in order to learn."

3. I'll wake up in the morning and say, "Okay, Natalie, you have until ten a.m. to do whatever you want. At ten you must have your hand on the pen." I give myself some space and an outside limit.

4. I wake up in the morning, and without thinking, washing, talking to anyone, I go right to my desk and begin writing.

5. These past two months I have been teaching all day, five days a week. I come home very tired and resistant to writing. There is a wonderful croissant place three blocks from my house that makes the best homemade chocolate-chip cookies for thirty cents. They also let you sit there and write forever. About an hour after I am home from work I say to myself, "Okay, Natalie,

if you go to the Croissant Express and write for an hour, you can have two chocolate-chip cookies." I am usually out the door within fifteen minutes since chocolate is one of my driving forces. One problem: on Friday I had the nerve to have four cookies instead of my quota of two, but anything to get me writing. Usually, once I'm in the midst of actually writing, it's its own greatest reward.

6. I try to fill a notebook a month. There's no quota on quality, just quantity—a full notebook, no matter what garbage I write. If it is the 25th of the month and I have only filled five pages and there are seventy more to fill by the end of the month, I have a lot of writing ahead of me in the next five days.

You can make up all kinds of friendly tricks. Just don't get caught in the endless cycle of guilt, avoidance, and pressure. When it is your time to write, write.

Trouble with the Editor

THE MORE CLEARLY you know the editor, the better you can ignore it. After a while, like the jabbering of an old drunk fool, it becomes just prattle in the background. Don't reinforce its power by listening to its empty words. If the voice says, "You are boring," and you listen to it and stop your hand from writing, that reinforces and gives credence to your editor. That voice knows that the term boring will stop you dead in your tracks, so you'll hear yourself saying that a lot about your writing. Hear "You are boring" as distant white laundry flapping in the breeze. Eventually it will dry up and someone miles away will fold it and take it in. Meanwhile you will continue to write.

Elkton, Minnesota: Whatever's in Front of You

I WALK INTO THE classroom in Elkton, Minnesota. Early April the fields around the school are wet, unplowed, not seeded yet. And the sky is deep gray. I tell the twenty-five eighth-graders that I am a Jew after I hear that *rabbis* is one of their spelling words. None of them has ever seen a Jew before. I am aware that everything I do now for the next hour represents "Jew." I walk in eating an apple: all Jews now will eat apples. I tell them I have never lived in a small town: now no Jew has ever lived in the country. One student asked if I knew anyone in a concentration camp. And we talk about the Germans: many are of German descent.

They are very warm and there's a beautiful depth of vulnerability about them. They know what well the water they drink comes from, that their cat who ran away two years ago will not return, how their hair feels against their heads as they run. I don't have to give them any rules about poetry. They live in that place already. Close to things. So I ask them, "Where do you come from, who are you, what makes you?" I tell them I'm from the city but I know these fields. In writing you can know everything. You can be here and know the streets of New York. You can have parts of others live in you: "I am the wing of the crow that left and will not return."

So this is one way to generate writing. I didn't have a plan before I went into class. I tried to be present, unafraid, open, and the situation gave me the subject. I know this is true wherever I go. The trick is to keep your heart open. In an inner-city school in downtown Manhattan I might come to a class armored with all kinds of ready-to-fix writing exercises, because I would be more scared. I was brought up in New York and have heard many stories. That would be a loss for everyone, mostly for myself. If I'm afraid, my writing's bent, untruthful to what is real. "But there is cause for fear there!" No, that's going in with a preconceived idea.

When I first graduated college in 1970, I worked as a substitute teacher for the Detroit public school system. It was after the race riots, and there were strong feelings of black power emanating from the students. I was naive, freshly moved to Detroit. Everything was new and I was open. I remember being called to substitute for an English class in an all-black high school. "Great," I thought. I had been an English major in college. I grabbed my frayed hardcover copy of *The Norton Anthology of English Literature* and drove to my school assignment. The eleventh-graders entered the classroom at the sounding of the bell—"Hey, girl, what you doin' here?" It was obvious that they weren't going to dutifully sit in their seats, but I didn't care.

This was English class and I was in love with literature. "Now, wait a minute. I want to share these poems with you. I love them." I read them my favorite, "God's Grandeur" by Gerard Manley Hopkins, which I had often read aloud in college to the dismay of my roommates. I read it to the Detroit English class with that same energy. They were totally silent after I read. Then a student grabbed a book of poems by Langston Hughes, shoved it at me, and said, "Read these." For the whole fifty minutes we read aloud black poets that the students wanted to hear.

Writers, when they write, need to approach things for the first time each time. A teacher in Elkton called me to the side: "Look under the desks. There's mud on the floor from their shoes. That's a good sign. It means spring." And I look in wonder for the first time.

How to generate writing ideas, things to write about? Whatever's in front of you is a good beginning. Then move out into all streets. You can go anyplace. Tell me everything you know. Don't worry if what you know you can't prove or haven't studied. I know the fields around Elkton because I say I do and because I want to walk out into them forever. Don't worry that forever might be the one week you're there as resident poet or salesman for a tractor company or a traveler on the way west. Own anything you want in your writing and then let it go.

Tap the Water Table

D ON'T WORRY ABOUT your talent or capability: that will grow as you practice. Katagiri Roshi said, "Capability is like a water table below the surface of earth." No one owns it, but you can tap it. You tap it with your effort and it will come through you. So just practice writing, and when you learn to trust your voice, direct it. If you want to write a novel, write a novel. If it's essays you want or short stories, write them. In the process of writing them, you will learn how. You can have the confidence that you will gradually acquire the technique and craft you need.

Instead people often begin writing from a poverty mentality. They are empty and they run to teachers and classes to learn about writing. We learn writing by doing it. That simple. We don't learn by going outside ourselves to authorities we think know about it. I had a lovely fat friend once who decided he wanted to start exercising. He went to a bookstore to find a book so he could read about it! You don't read about exercise to lose weight. You exercise to lose those pounds.

The terrible thing about public schools is they take young children who are natural poets and story writers and have them read literature and then step away from it and talk "about" it.

The Red Wheelbarrow
BY WILLIAM CARLOS WILLIAMS

so much depends
upon

a red wheel
barrow

glazed with rain
water

beside the white
   chickens[4]

"What did the poet mean by the 'red wheelbarrow'? Did he mean a sunset? A chariot? And why was it 'glazed with rain'?" So many questions. He meant nothing so much as a wheelbarrow, and it was red because it was red and it had just rained. So much depends on it because poems are small moments of enlightenment—at that moment the wheelbarrow just as it was woke Williams up and was everything.

Poems are taught as though the poet has put a secret key in his words and it is the reader's job to find it. Poems are not mystery novels. Instead we should go closer and closer to the work. Learn to recall images and lines precisely as the writer said them. Don't step away from their warmth and fire to talk "about" them. Stay close to them. That's how you'll learn to write. Stay with the original work. Stay with your original mind and write from it.

We Are Not the Poem

THE PROBLEM IS we think we exist. We think our words are permanent and solid and stamp us forever. That's not true. We write in the moment. Sometimes when I read poems at a reading to strangers, I realize they think those poems are me. They are not me, even if I speak in the "I" person. They were my thoughts and my hand and the space and the emotions at that time of writing. Watch yourself. Every minute we change. It is a great opportunity. At any point, we can step out of our frozen selves and our ideas and begin fresh. That is how writing is. Instead of freezing us, it frees us.

The ability to put something down—to tell how you feel about an old husband, an old shoe, or the memory of a cheese sandwich on a gray morning in Miami—that moment you can finally align how you feel inside with the words you write; at that moment you are free because you are not fighting those things inside. You have accepted them, become one with them. I have a poem entitled "No Hope"—it's a long poem. I always think of it as joyous because in my ability to write of desperation and emptiness I felt alive again and unafraid. However, when I read it, people comment, "How sad." I try to explain, but no one listens.

It is important to remember we are not the poem. People will react however they want; and if you write poetry, get used to no reaction at all. But that's okay. The power is always in the act of writing. Come back to that again and again and again. Don't get caught in the admiration for your poems. It's fun. But then the public makes you read their favorites over and over until you get sick of those poems. Write good poems and let go of them. Publish them, read them, go on writing.

I remember Galway Kinnell when his wonderful *Book of Nightmares* first came out. It was a Thursday afternoon in Ann Arbor. I'd never heard of him, much less could I pronounce his name. He sang those poems; they were new and exciting for him and a great accomplishment. Six years later I heard him read again at St. John's in Santa Fe, New Mexico. He'd read that book so much in those six years that he was sick of it. He ran through the poems, put down the book, and said, "Where's the party?" There was nothing dangerous for him in them anymore. The air was no longer electric.

It is very painful to become frozen with your poems, to gain too much recognition for a certain set of poems. The real life is in writing, not in reading the same ones over and over again for years. We constantly need new insights, visions. We don't exist in any solid form.

There is no permanent truth you can corner in a poem that will satisfy you forever. Don't identify too strongly with your work. Stay fluid behind those black-and-white words. They are not you. They were a great moment going through you. A moment you were awake enough to write down and capture.

Man Eats Car

THERE WAS AN article in the newspaper several years ago—I did not read it, it was told to me—about a yogi in India who ate a car. Not all at once, but slowly over a year's time. Now, I like a story like that. How much weight did he gain? How old was he? Did he have a full set of teeth? Even the carburetor, the steering wheel, the radio? What make was the car? Did he drink the oil?

I told this story to a group of third-graders in Owatonna, Minnesota. They were sitting on the blue carpet in front of me. The students looked confused and asked the most obvious question, "Why did he eat a car?," and then they commented, "Ugh!" But there was one bristling, brown-eyed student, who will be my friend forever, who just looked at me and burst into tremendous laughter, and I began laughing too. It was fantastic! A man had eaten a car! Right from the beginning there is no logic in it. It is absurd.

In a sense, this is how we should write. Not asking "Why?," not delicately picking among candies (or spark plugs), but voraciously, letting our minds eat up everything and spewing it out on paper with great energy. We shouldn't think, "This is a good subject for writing." "This we shouldn't talk about." Writing is everything, unconditional. There is no separation between writing, life, and the mind. If you think big enough to let people eat cars, you will be able to see that ants are elephants and men are women. You will be able to see the transparency of all forms so that all separations disappear.

This is what metaphor is. It is not saying that an ant is *like* an elephant. Perhaps; both are alive. No. Metaphor is saying the ant *is* an elephant. Now, logically speaking, I know there is a difference. If you put elephants and ants before me, I believe that every time I will correctly identify the elephant and the ant. So metaphor must come from a very different place than that of the logical, intelligent mind. It comes from a place that is very courageous, willing to step out of our preconceived ways of seeing things and open so large that it can see the oneness in an ant and in an elephant.

But don't worry about metaphors. Don't think, "I have to write metaphors to sound literary." First of all, don't be literary. Metaphors cannot be forced. If all of you does not believe that the elephant and the ant are one at the moment you write it, it will sound false. If all of you does believe it, there are some who might consider you crazy; but it's better to be crazy than false. But how do you make your mind believe it and write metaphor?

Don't "make" your mind do anything. Simply step out of the way and record your thoughts as they roll through you. Writing practice softens the heart and mind, helps to keep us flexible so that rigid distinctions between apples and milk, tigers and celery, disappear. We can step through moons right into bears. You will take leaps naturally if you follow your thoughts, because the mind spontaneously takes great leaps. You know. Have you ever been able to just stay with one thought for very long? Another one arises.

Your mind is leaping, your writing will leap, but it won't be artificial. It will reflect the nature of first thoughts, the way we see the world when we are free from prejudice and can see the underlying principles. We are all connected. Metaphor knows this and therefore is religious. There is no separation between ants and elephants. All boundaries disappear, as though we were looking through rain or squinting our eyes at city lights.

Writing Is Not a McDonald's Hamburger

S OMETIMES I HAVE a student who is really good right from the beginning. I'm thinking of one in particular. The air was electric when he read, and he was often shaking. The writing process split him open; he was able to tell about being fourteen years old in a mental hospital, about walking the streets of Minneapolis tripping on LSD, about sitting next to the dead body of his brother in San Francisco. He said he had wanted to write for years. People told him he should be a writer, but anytime he sat down to write he couldn't connect the words on paper with the event or his feelings.

That is because he had an idea of what he wanted to say before he came to paper. Of course, you can sit down and have something you want to say. But then you must let its expression be born in you and on the paper. Don't hold too tight; allow it to come out how it needs to rather than trying to control it. Yes, those experiences, memories, feelings, are in us, but you can't carry them out on paper whole the way a cook brings out a pizza from the oven.

Let go of everything when you write, and try at a simple beginning with simple words to express what you have inside. It won't begin smoothly. Allow yourself to be awkward. You are stripping yourself. You are exposing your life, not how your ego would like to see you represented, but how you are as a human being. And it is because of this that I think writing is religious. It splits you open and softens your heart toward the homely world.

When I'm cranky now, miserable, dissatisfied, pessimistic, negative, generally rotten, I recognize it as a feeling. I know the feeling can change. I know it is energy that wants to find a place in the world and wants friends.

But yes, you can have topics you want to write about—"I want to write about my brother who died in San Francisco"—but come to it not with your mind and ideas, but with your whole body—your heart and gut and arms. Begin to write in the dumb, awkward way an animal cries out in pain, and there you will find your intelligence, your words, your voice.

People often say, "I was walking along [or driving, shopping, jogging] and I had this whole poem go through my mind, but when I sat down to write it, I couldn't get it to come out right." I never can either. Sitting to write is another activity. Let go of walking or jogging and the poem that was born then in your mind. This is another moment. Write another poem. Perhaps secretly hope something of what you thought a while ago might come out, but let it come out however it does. Don't force it.

The same student mentioned above was so excited about writing that he immediately tried to form a book. I told him, "Take it slow. Just let yourself write for a while. Learn what that is about." Writing is a whole lifetime and a lot of practice. I understood his urgency. We want to think we are doing something useful, going someplace, achieving something—"I am writing a book."

Give yourself some space before you decide to write those big volumes. Learn to trust the force of your own voice. Naturally, it will evolve a direction and a need for one, but it will come from a different place than your need to be an achiever. Writing is not a McDonald's hamburger. The cooking is slow, and in the beginning you are not sure whether a roast or a banquet or a lamb chop will be the result.

Obsessions

E VERY ONCE IN a while I make a list of my obsessions. Some obsessions change and there are
always more. Some are thankfully forgotten.

Writers end up writing about their obsessions.
Things that haunt them; things they can't forget; stories they carry in their bodies waiting to be released.

I have my writing groups make lists of their obsessions so that they can see what they unconsciously
(and consciously) spend their waking hours thinking
about. After you write them down you can put them
to good use. You have a list of things to write about.
And your main obsessions have power; they are what
you will come back to in your writing over and over
again. And you'll create new stories around them. So
you might as well give in to them. They probably take
over your life whether you want them to or not, so
you ought to get them to work for you.

One of my obsessions is my Jewish family. Every
once in a while I decide I've written enough about
them. I don't want to sound like a momma's girl.
There are other things in the world to write about. It
is true that there are other topics and they do come
up naturally, but when I have made a conscious

decision to not write about my family, the act of repressing it seems to repress everything else too, simply because I am spending a lot of energy avoiding something.

It's like when I decide to go on a diet. Right after I make that decision, food seems to be the only real thing on earth, and as I drive the car, run down the block, write in my journal—all these actions become ways of avoiding the one thing I suddenly really want. For me, it works better to give food and hunger a space in my life, but in a friendly way so that I don't destructively devour twelve cookies at a time.

Just so with writing about my family. Give them a few pages and they will take their place in the Hall of Obsessions and allow me space for other topics. Try to squelch them and they turn the corner in every one-horse-town poem I've ever written—even an Iowa farm wife begins to sound like she's about to make blintzes.

I learned once from a recovering alcoholic that at parties alcoholics always know where the liquor is, how much there is, how much they've drunk, and where they are going to get their next drink. I have never cared that much about liquor, but I know I love chocolate. After hearing about an alcoholic's behavior, I watched myself. The next day I was at a friend's. His roommate was making brownies. We had to go to a show before the brownies were out of the oven. I was aware that subtly throughout the whole movie I was thinking about those brownies. I couldn't wait to get back and have one. When the show was finished, we coincidentally met some friends who suggested that we go out some place to talk. I saw myself get panicky: I wanted those brownies. I made up a quick excuse why we had to return to my friend's house before we went on with the evening.

We are run by our compulsions. Maybe it's just me. But it seems that obsessions have power. Harness that power. I know most of my writing friends are obsessed with writing. It works in the same way as chocolate does. We're always thinking we should be writing no matter what else we might be doing. It's not fun. The life of an artist isn't easy. You're never free unless you are doing your art. But I guess doing art is better than drinking a lot or filling up with chocolate. I often wonder if all the writers who are alcoholics drink a lot because they aren't writing or are having trouble writing. It is not because they are writers that they are drinking, but because they are writers who are not writing.

There is freedom in being a writer and writing. It is fulfilling your function. I used to think freedom meant doing whatever you want. It means knowing who you are, what you are supposed to be doing on this earth, and then simply doing it. It is not getting sidetracked, thinking you shouldn't write any more about your Jewish family when that's your role in life: to record their history, who they were in Brooklyn, on Long

Island, at Miami Beach—the first generation of American Goldbergs—before it all passes and is gone.

Katagiri Roshi says: "Poor artists. They suffer very much. They finish a masterpiece and they are not satisfied. They want to go on and do another." Yes, but it's better to go on and do another if you have the urge than to start drinking and become an alcoholic or eat a pound of good fudge and get fat.

So perhaps not all obsessions are bad. An obsession for peace is good. But then be peaceful. Don't just think about it. An obsession for writing is good. But then write. Don't let it get twisted into drinking. An obsession for chocolate is not good. I know. It's unhealthy and doesn't help the world the way peace and writing do.

Carolyn Forché, a poet who won the Lamont Poetry Award for her book *The Country Between Us,* about El Salvador, said, "Change your innermost obsessions to become a political writer." That makes sense. You don't write about politics by *thinking* you should. That will become doggerel. Start caring about politics, reading about it, talking about it, and don't worry about what it will do to your writing. When it becomes an obsession, you will naturally write about it.

Original Detail

T HOUGH THIS IS a short chapter, it is an important one: use original detail in your writing. Life is so rich, if you can write down the real details of the way things were and are, you hardly need anything else. Even if you transplant the beveled windows, slow-rotating Rheingold sign, Wise potato chip rack, and tall red stools from the Aero Tavern that you drank in in New York into a bar in a story in another state and time, the story will have authenticity and groundedness. "Oh, no, that bar was on Long Island, I can't put it in New Jersey"—yes, you can. You don't have to be rigid about original detail. The imagination is capable of detail transplants, but using the details you actually know and have seen will give your writing believability and truthfulness. It creates a good solid foundation from which you can build.

Naturally, if you have just been to New Orleans in the dripping August heat and have sucked the fat out of the heads of crayfish at the Magnolia Bar on St. Charles Avenue, you can't have the thick-wristed character in your story in Cleveland on a January night doing the same thing at his local bar. It won't work, unless, of course, you are moving into surrealism, where all boundaries begin to melt.

Be awake to the details around you, but don't be self-conscious. "Okay. I'm at a wedding. The bride has on blue. The groom is wearing a red carnation. They are serving chopped liver on doilies." Relax, enjoy the wedding, be present with an open heart. You will naturally take in your environment, and later, sitting at your desk, you will be able to recall just how it was dancing with the bride's redheaded mother, seeing the bit of red lipstick smeared on her front tooth when she smiled, and smelling her perfume mixed with perspiration.

The Power of Detail

I AM IN Costa's Chocolate Shop in Owatonna, Minnesota. My friend is opposite me. We've just finished Greek salads and are writing in our notebooks for a half hour among glasses of water, a half-sipped Coke, and a cup of coffee with milk. The booths are orange, and near the front counter are lines of cream candies dipped in chocolate. Across the street is the Owatonna Bank, designed by Louis Sullivan, Frank Lloyd Wright's teacher. Inside the bank is a large cow mural and beautiful stained-glass windows.

Our lives are at once ordinary and mythical. We live and die, age beautifully or full of wrinkles. We wake in the morning, buy yellow cheese, and hope we have enough money to pay for it. At the same instant we have these magnificent hearts that pump through all sorrow and all winters we are alive on the earth. We are important and our lives are important, magnificent really, and their details are worthy to be recorded. This is how writers must think, this is how we must sit down with pen in hand. We were here; we are human beings; this is how we lived. Let it be known, the earth passed before us. Our details are important. Otherwise, if they are not, we can drop a bomb and it doesn't matter.

Yad Vashem, a memorial for the Holocaust, is in Jerusalem. It has a whole library that catalogs the names of the six million martyrs. Not only did the library have their names, it also had where they lived, were born, anything that could be found out about them. These people existed and they mattered. *Yad Vashem,* as a matter of fact, actually means "memorial to the name." It was not nameless masses that were slaughtered; they were human beings.

Likewise, in Washington, D.C., there is the Vietnam Memorial. There are fifty thousand names listed—middle names, too—of American soldiers killed in Vietnam. Real human beings with names were killed and their breaths moved out of this world. There was the name of Donald Miller, my second-grade friend who drew tanks, soldiers, and ships in the margins of all his math papers. Seeing names makes us remember. A name is what we carry all our life, and we respond to its call in a classroom, to its pronunciation at a graduation, or to our name whispered in the night.

It is important to say the names of who we are, the names of the places we have lived, and to write the details of our lives. "I lived on Coal Street in Albuquerque next to a garage and carried paper bags of groceries down Lead Avenue. One person had planted beets early that spring, and I watched their red/green leaves grow."

We have lived; our moments are important. This is what it is to be a writer: to be the carrier of details that make up history, to care about the orange booths in the coffee shop in Owatonna.

Recording the details of our lives is a stance against bombs with their mass ability to kill, against too much speed and efficiency. A writer must say yes to life, to all of life: the water glasses, the Kemp's half-and-half, the ketchup on the counter. It is not a writer's task to say, "It is dumb to live in a small town or to eat in a café when you can eat macrobiotic at home." Our task is to say a holy yes to the real things of our life as they exist—the real truth of who we are: several pounds overweight, the gray, cold street outside, the Christmas tinsel in the showcase, the Jewish writer in the orange booth across from her blond friend who has black children. We must become writers who accept things as they are, come to love the details, and step forward with a yes on our lips so there can be no more noes in the world, noes that invalidate life and stop these details from continuing.

Baking a Cake

WHEN YOU BAKE a cake, you have ingredients: sugar, flour, butter, baking soda, eggs, milk. You put them in a bowl and mix them up, but this does not make a cake. This makes goop. You have to put them in the oven and add heat or energy to transform it into cake, and the cake looks nothing like its original ingredients. It's a lot like parents unable to claim their hippie kids as their own in the sixties. Milk and eggs look at their pound cake and say, "Not ours." Not egg, not milk, but Ph.D. daughter of refugee parents—a foreigner in her own home.

In a sense this is what writing is like. You have all these ingredients, the details of your life, but just to list them is not enough. "I was born in Brooklyn. I have a mother and a father. I am female." You must add the heat and energy of your heart. This is not just any father; this is your father. The character who smoked cigars and put too much ketchup on his steak. The one you loved and hated. You can't just mix the ingredients in a bowl; they have no life. You must become one with the details in love or hate; they become an extension of your body. Nabokov says, "Caress the divine details." He doesn't say, "Jostle them in place or bang them around." *Caress* them, touch them tenderly. Care about what is around you. Let your whole body touch the river you are writing about, so if you call it yellow or stupid or slow, all of you is feeling it. There should be no separate you when you are deeply engaged. Katagiri Roshi said: "When you do zazen [sitting meditation], you should be gone. So zazen does zazen. Not Steve or Barbara does zazen." This is also how you should be when you write: writing does writing. You disappear: you are simply recording the thoughts that are streaming through you.

The cake is baking in the oven. All that heat goes into the making of that cake. The heat is not distracted, thinking, "Oh, I wanted it to be a chocolate cake, not a pound cake." You don't think as you write, "Oh, I don't like my life, I should have been born in Illinois." You don't think. You accept what is and put down its truth. Katagiri Roshi has said: "Literature will tell you what life is, but it won't tell you how to get out of it."

Ovens can be very cantankerous sometimes, and you might have to learn ways to turn your heat on. Timing your writing adds pressure and helps to heat things up and blast through the internal censor. Also, keeping your hand moving and not stopping add to the heat, so a beautiful cake may rise out of the mixture of your daily details. If you find yourself checking the clock too much as you write, say to yourself you are going to keep writing until three (or four or five) pages, both sides, are filled or until the cake is baked, however long that takes. And you are never sure once the heat begins whether you will get a devil's food or an angel food cake. There are no guarantees; don't worry. They're both good to eat.

There are people who try to use heat only, without ingredients, to make a cake. The heat is cozy and feels good, but when you're done, there's not much there for anyone else to eat. That's usually abstract writing: we get a sense there is great warmth there, but we have nothing to bite into. If you use details, you become better skilled at conveying your ecstasy or sorrow. So while you fly around in the heat of the oven, bring in the batter in the pan so we know exactly what your feelings taste like, so we may be a gourmet of them: "Oh, it's a pound cake, a brownie, a light lemon soufflé." That is what her feelings feel like. Not "It was great, it was great!" Yes, it was great, but how great? Give us the flavor. In other words, use details. They are the basic unit of writing.

And in using them, you are not only baking cakes and buzzing around the oven. In writing with detail, you are turning to face the world. It is a deeply political act, because you are not just staying in the heat of your own emotions. You are offering up some good solid bread for the hungry.

Living Twice

WRITERS LIVE TWICE. They go along with their regular life, are as fast as anyone in the grocery store, crossing the street, getting dressed for work in the morning. But there's another part of them that they have been training. The one that lives everything a second time. That sits down and sees their life again and goes over it. Looks at the texture and details.

In a rainstorm, everyone quickly runs down the street with umbrellas, raincoats, newspapers over their heads. Writers go back outside in the rain with a notebook in front of them and a pen in hand. They look at the puddles, watch them fill, watch the rain splash in them. You can say a writer practices being dumb. Only a dummy would stand out in the rain and watch a puddle. If you're smart, you get in out of the rain so you won't catch cold, and you have health insurance, in case you get sick. If you're dumb, you are more interested in the puddle than in your security and insurance or in getting to work on time.

You're more interested, finally, in living life again in your writing than in making money. Now, let's understand—writers do like money; artists, contrary to popular belief, do like to eat. It's only that money isn't the driving force. I feel very rich when I have time to write and very poor when I get a regular paycheck and no time to work at my real work. Think of it. Employers pay salaries for time. That is the basic commodity that human beings have that is valuable. We exchange our time in life for money. Writers stay with the first step—their time—and feel it is valuable even before they get money for it. They hold on to it and aren't so eager to sell it. It's like inheriting land from your family. It's always been in your family: they have always owned it. Someone comes along and wants to buy it. Writers, if they are smart, won't sell too much of it. They know once it's sold, they might be able to buy a second car, but there will be no place they can go to sit still, no place to dream on.

So it is good to be a little dumb when you want to write. You carry that slow person inside you who needs time; it keeps you from selling it all away. That person will need a place to go and will demand to stare into rain puddles in the rain, usually with no hat on, and to feel the drops on her scalp.

Writers Have Good Figures

WHAT PEOPLE DON'T realize is that writing is physical. It doesn't have to do with thought alone. It has to do with sight, smell, taste, feeling, with everything being alive and activated. The rule for writing practice of "keeping your hand moving," not stopping, actually is a way to physically break through your mental resistances and cut through the concept that writing is just about ideas and thinking. You are physically engaged with the pen, and your hand, connected to your arm, is pouring out the record of your senses. There is no separation between the mind and body; therefore, you can break through the mind barriers to writing through the physical act of writing, just as you can believe with your mind that your hand won't stop at the wood, so you can break a board in karate.

After one writing class a student, in amazement, said, "Oh, I get it! Writing is a visual art!" Yes, and it's a kinesthetic, visceral art too. I've told fourth-graders that my writing hand could knock out Muhammad Ali. They believed me because they know it is true. Sixth-graders are older and more skeptical. I've had to prove it to them by putting my fist through their long gray lockers.

When I look around at people writing, I can tell just by their physical posture if they have broken through or not. If they did, their teeth are rattling around in their mouth, no longer tight in their gums; their hearts might be pounding hard or aching. They are breathing deeply. Their handwriting is looser, more generous, and their bodies are relaxed enough to run for miles. This is why I say all writers, no matter how fat, thin, or flabby, have good figures. They are always working out. Remember this. They are in tune, toned up, in rhythm with the hills, the highway, and can go for long stretches and many miles of paper. They move with grace in and out of many worlds.

And what great writers actually pass on is not so much their words, but they hand on their breath at their moments of inspiration. If you read a great poem aloud—for example, "To a Skylark" by Percy Bysshe Shelley—and read it the way he set it up and punctuated it, what you are doing is breathing his inspired breath at the moment he wrote that poem. That breath was so powerful it still can be awakened in us over 150 years later. Taking it on is very exhilarating. This is why it is good to remember: if you want to get high, don't drink whiskey; read Shakespeare, Tennyson, Keats, Neruda, Hopkins, Millay, Whitman, aloud and let your body sing.

Listening

A T SIX YEARS OLD I was sitting at my cousin's piano in Brooklyn making believe I was playing a song and singing along with it: "In the gloaming, oh my darling . . ." My cousin, who was nine years older, sat down beside me on the piano stool and screamed to my mother, "Aunt Sylvia, Natalie is tone-deaf. She can't sing!" From then on, I never sang and I rarely listened to music. When I heard the scores from Broadway shows on radio, I just learned the words and never tried to imitate the melody. As I grew older my friends and I played a game, Name That Tune. I would hum something and they would break into peals of laughter, not possibly believing I was actually humming "Younger Than Springtime" from South Pacific. This was a way I received attention, though my young heart secretly longed to be Gypsy Rose Lee. After all, I knew all the words to all the songs. But basically, the world of music was not available to me. I was tone-deaf: I had a physical defect, like a missing foot or finger.

Several years ago I took a singing lesson from a Sufi singing master, and he told me there is no such thing as tone-deafness. "Singing is 90 percent listening. You have to learn to listen." If you listen totally, your body fills with the music, so when you open your mouth the music automatically comes out of you. A few weeks after that, I sang in tune with a friend for the first time in my life and thought for sure I had become enlightened. My individual voice disappeared and our two voices became one.

Writing, too, is 90 percent listening. You listen so deeply to the space around you that it fills you, and when you write, it pours out of you. If you can capture that reality around you, your writing needs nothing else. You don't only listen to the person speaking to you across the table, but simultaneously listen to the air, the chair, and the door. And go beyond the door. Take in the sound of the season, the sound of the color coming in through the windows. Listen to the past, future, and present right where you are. Listen with your whole body, not only with your ears, but with your hands, your face, and the back of your neck.

Listening is receptivity. The deeper you can listen, the better you can write. You take in the way things are without judgment, and the next day you can write the truth about the way things are. Jack Kerouac in his list of prose essentials said, "Be submissive to everything. Open. Listening." He also said, "No time for poetry, but exactly what is." If you can capture the way things are, that's all the poetry you'll ever need.

Rabbi Zalman Schachter once told a group of people at the Lama Foundation that when he was in rabbinical school the students were not allowed to take notes. They had to just listen, and when the lecture was done they were expected to know it. The idea was that we can remember everything. We choose and have trained our minds to repress things.

After something is read in class, I often have the students do a "recall": "As close as you can to the exact words of what was said or written, repeat anything that was strong for you. Don't step away and say, 'I liked when she talked about the farmland.' Give us exact details: 'Standing in the field, I was lonelier than a crow.'" Besides opening and receiving what was said, this kind of deep, nonevaluative listening awakens stories and images inside you. By listening in this way you become a clear mirror to reflect reality, your reality and the reality around you.

Basically, if you want to become a good writer, you need to do three things. Read a lot, listen well and deeply, and write a lot. And don't think too much. Just enter the heat of words and sounds and colored sensations and keep your pen moving across the page.

If you read good books, when you write, good books will come out of you. Maybe it's not quite that easy, but if you want to learn something, go to the source. Basho, the great seventeenth-century Haiku master, said, "If you want to know about a tree, go to the tree." If you want to know poetry, read it, listen to it. Let those patterns and forms be imprinted in you. Don't step away from poetry to analyze a poem with your logical mind. Enter poetry with your whole body. Dogen, a great Zen master, said, "If you walk in the mist, you get wet." So just listen, read, and write. Little by little, you will come closer to what you need to say and express it through your voice.

Be patient and don't worry about it. Just sing and write in tune.

Don't Marry the Fly

W ATCH WHEN YOU listen to a piece of writing. There might be spaces where your mind wanders. We sometimes respond with comments such as "I don't know, it got too deep for me" or "There was just too much description, I couldn't follow it." Often the problem is not in the reader but in the writing.

These are places where the writer went back on himself, became diverted in his own mind's enjoyment, forgetting where the story was originally heading.

A writer might be writing about a restaurant scene but become obsessed with the fly on the napkin and begin to describe, in minute detail, the fly's back, the fly's dreams, its early childhood, its technique for flying through screen windows. The reader or listener becomes lost because right before that the waiter had come to the table in the writing and the listener is waiting for him to serve the food. Also, the writer may not be clear on his true direction or not directly present with his material. This creates a blur in the writing. It is some area that is fuzzy and so loses the reader's attention because it makes a little gap, letting the reader's mind wander away from the work.

A responsibility of literature is to make people awake, present, alive. If the writer wanders, then the reader, too, will wander. The fly on the table might be part of the whole description of a restaurant. It might be appropriate to tell precisely the sandwich that it just walked over, but there is a fine line between precision and self-indulgence.

Stay on the side of precision; know your goal and stay present with it. If your mind and writing wander from it, bring them gently back. When we write, many avenues open up inside us. Don't get too far afield. Stay with the details and with your direction. Don't be self-absorbed, which eventually creates vague, muddy writing. We might really get to know the fly but forget where we are: the restaurant, the rain outside, the friend across the table. The fly is important, but it has its place. Don't ignore the fly; don't become obsessed with it. Irving Howe wrote in his introduction to *Jewish American Stories* that the best art *almost* becomes sentimental but doesn't. Recognize the fly, even love it if you want, but don't marry it.

Don't Use Writing
to Get Love

About five years ago a friend was mugged on the Lower East Side of Manhattan. She told me later that she threw up her arms and immediately yelled, "Don't kill me, I'm a writer!" "How odd," I thought at the time. "Why did she think that would save her?"

Writers get confused. We think writing gives us an excuse for being alive. We forget that being alive is unconditional and that life and writing are two separate entities. Often we use writing as a way to receive notice, attention, love. "See what I wrote. I must be a good person." We *are* good people before we ever write a word.

A few years ago, after every reading I gave, no matter how well everyone appreciated my work, I felt lonely and terrible. I blamed it on my writing. It wasn't my work that was the problem. I was going through a divorce and had very low self-esteem. *I* needed support—not my poetry. I confused the two. I forgot that I am not the poem. The poems were healthy; I wasn't. *I* needed care. From then on I always invited a friend to be my "date" at public events. I told the friend that as soon as I was finished reading, "Come right up to me, hug me, tell me how beautiful I looked and how wonderful I am. I don't care if I totally bombed out that night. Tell me I am wonderful." A week later I can take a close look at my performance. That night, "Tell me I'm wonderful."

As writers we are always seeking support. First we should notice that we are already supported every moment. There is the earth below our feet and there is the air, filling our lungs and emptying them. We should begin from this when we need support. There is the sunlight coming through the window and the silence of the morning. Begin from these. Then turn to face a friend and feel how good it is when she says, "I love your work." Believe her as you believe the floor will hold you up, the chair will let you sit.

I had a student who sent me two short stories to read, and then the following week we had an hour-long conference. I hadn't worked with her in a year and a half, and I was impressed by her progress. I told her, "The stories are complete, touching, very beautiful." I began to notice about twenty minutes into the conference that she was becoming angry. "I think you are charging me too much." What she was really saying was, "You haven't done your work. You didn't spend time ripping them apart. I didn't come here to hear compliments. These couldn't possibly be so good. You are exaggerating." "Listen, you have to believe me. This is terrific work. It's ready for publication." I suggested she send it out. Within a month one of the stories was accepted by a very fine magazine. Not only was she paid, but they told her that they had recently decided to stop publishing short stories, but "This was so good, we changed our minds."

We want honest support and encouragement. When we receive it, we don't believe it, but we are quick to accept criticism to reinforce our deepest beliefs that, in truth, we are no good and not really writers. My ex-husband used to say to me, "You look ugly. Aah, now that I have your attention . . ." He said when he complimented me, I never heard him, but as soon as he said something negative, I perked right up.

Students say to me, "Well, you're just the teacher. You have to say something positive." Friends say, "Well, you're just my friend. You already like me." *Stop!* Really stop when someone is complimenting you. Even if it's painful and you are not used to it, just keep breathing, listen, and let yourself take it in. *Feel* how good it is. Build up a tolerance for positive, honest support.

What Are Your Deep Dreams?

I ASKED MY Sunday-night group (many of whom had been doing practice writing for three years), "Where do you want to go with writing? You have this strong creative voice; you've been able to separate out the creator and editor. What do you want to do with it?"

There comes a time to shape and direct the force we have learned. I asked them, "What are your deep dreams? Write for five minutes." Many of us don't know, don't recognize, avoid our deep dreams. When we write for five, ten minutes we are forced to put down wishes that float around in our mind and that we might not pay attention to. It is an opportunity to write down, without thinking, wishes at the periphery of our perceptions.

Reread them. Start to take your dreams and wishes seriously. If you're not sure, if you honestly don't know what you want to do, start wishing for a direction, for your way to appear.

When I was in Israel last year, I walked the streets of Jerusalem wondering what other kind of writing I should do. I was finishing my second manuscript of poetry, *Top of My Lungs,* and knew that I needed something, some new form. Lots of poets back in the Twin Cities were writing novels. Judith Guest's success with *Ordinary People,* her first novel, spurred everyone on (she lives in Edina, Minnesota). I kept saying to myself, "Natalie, do you want to write a novel?" The answer was clearly "No!" There was some comfort in that, in knowing what I didn't want. But I was worried. I had visions of my end, lying in the gutter, clutching a few last poems in my hand and, with my last breath, begging someone to read them.

There's a wonderful *New Yorker* cartoon of a man standing in front of passengers on a plane with a rifle and a notebook in his hands, saying, "Now, sit still. No one is going to be hurt. I just want you to listen to a few of my poems." Poetry has never been a favorite American pastime.

A friend who is a poet, now writing a mystery novel, suggested I write this book. I remembered that I had started it five years ago. The time wasn't right then, but like our obsessions, our dreams do reoccur. We might as well pay attention to them and act on them. It is a way to penetrate into our lives; otherwise we might drift with our dreams forever.

Once you have learned to trust your own voice and allowed that creative force inside you to come out, you can direct it to write short stories, novels, and poetry, do revisions, and so on. You have the basic tool to fulfill your writing dreams. But beware. This type of writing will uncover other dreams you have, too—going to Tibet, being the first woman president of the United States, building a solar studio in New Mexico—and they will be in black and white. It will be harder to avoid them.

Syntax

T RY THIS. Take one of your most boring pieces of
writing and choose from it three or four consecutive lines or sentences and write them at the top
of a blank piece of paper.

I can't write because I'm an ice cube and my
mouth goes dry and there's nothing to say and I'd
rather eat ice cream.

Okay. See each one of those words simply as wooden
blocks, all the same size and color. No noun or verb
has any more value than *the, a, and*. Everything is
equal. Now for about a third of a page scramble them
up as though you were just moving wooden blocks
around. Don't try to make any sense of what you
write down. Your mind will keep trying to construct
something. Hold back that urge, relax, and mind-
lessly write down the words. You will have to repeat
words to fill a third of a page.

Write I'm an mouth rather cream say eat ice and
nothing dry I an write rather say and my goes
cube because an there's I'd to dry goes write and

mouth cream to I'd rather dry cube I'm an write
I and nothing say goes an can't because nothing
rather I'd dry to and say cream goes ice rather to
my cube nothing there's say.

Now, if you would like, arbitrarily put in a few periods, a question mark, maybe an exclamation mark,
colons, or semicolons. Do all of this without thinking,
without trying to make any sense. Just for fun.

Write I'm an mouth rather cream. Say eat ice
and nothing dry! I an write rather say and; my
goes cube because an there's. I'd to dry goes
write and mouth cream to. I'd rather. Dry cube
I'm an write I and nothing say goes. An can't because nothing rather; I'd dry to and say cream
goes ice. Rather to my cube nothing there's say?

Now read it aloud as though it were saying something. Your voice should have inflection and expression. You might try reading it in an angry voice, an
exuberant, sad, whining, petulant, or demanding
voice, to help you get into it.

What have we done? Our language is usually
locked into a sentence syntax of subject/verb/direct-
object. There is a subject acting on an object. "I see
the dog"—with this sentence structure, "I" is the
center of the universe. We forget in our language

structure that while "I" looks at "the dog," "the dog" is simultaneously looking at us. It is interesting to note that in the Japanese language the sentence would say, "I dog seeing." There is an exchange or interaction rather than a subject acting on an object.

We think in sentences, and the way we think is the way we see. If we think in the structure subject/verb/direct-object, then that is how we form our world. By cracking open that syntax, we release energy and are able to see the world afresh and from a new angle. We stop being so chauvinistic as *Homo sapiens.* Other beings besides human beings matter on the earth: ants have their own cities; dogs have their own lives; cats are always busy rehearsing for a nap; plants breathe, trees have a longer life span than we do. It is true that we can have a sentence with a dog or cat or a fly as the subject—"The dog sees the cat"—but still there is the pattern of self-centeredness and egocentricity built into the very structure of our language. It is a terrible burden to have to be master. We are not ruling the world. It is an illusion, and the illusion of our syntax structure perpetuates it.

Katagiri Roshi used to say: "Have kind consideration for all sentient beings." Once I asked him, "What are sentient beings anyway? Are they things that feel?" He told me that we have to be kind even to the chair, the air, the paper, and the street. That's how big and accepting our minds have to become.

When Buddha reached enlightenment under the bodhi tree, he said: "I am now enlightened with all beings." He didn't say: "I am enlightened and you're not!" or "I see enlightenment" as though he were separate from it.

This does not mean that from now on we should remain immobilized because we are afraid of offending the rug below our feet or accidentally jolting a glass. It does not mean that we should not use our syntax structure because it is wrong. Only once you have done this exercise, though you probably will go back to sentences, there is a crack, a place where the wind of energy can fly through you. Though "I eat an artichoke" sounds sensible and people will think you are sane, you now know that behind that syntax structure, the artichoke happens to also be eating you and changing you forever, especially if you dip it in garlic-butter sauce and if you totally let the artichoke leaf taste your tongue! The more you are aware of the syntax you move, see, and write in, the better control you have and the more you can step out of it when you need to. Actually, by breaking open syntax, you often get closer to the truth of what you need to say.

Here are some examples of poems taken from *Shout, Applaud,* a collection of poems written at Norhaven, a residence for women who are mentally retarded.[5] These women were never solidly indoctrinated in English-language syntax, so these poems are good examples of what can be created outside of it. Also they are fresh in another way: they are full of surprise—because you had breakfast yesterday doesn't mean it isn't amazing to eat eggs today!

Give Me a White
BY MARION PINSKI

I love white
to write
to write my name.
Please give Marion
Pinski a white.
I like to white
because of write my name, I could.
I know how to spell it
correct.
I want white to write
my name with.
I like to write my name.
I'd like white, now.
I asked in a nice way.
I love white, I do.
To write, to write
my name, yes.
I got my own money, I do.
Trying to.

Maple Leaf
BY BETTY FREEMAN

That I dream the lady does to be young
and to be in her pretty red Christmas ball.
Her dress looks beautiful like a swan.
The swan floats with his thin white feathers
when his soft snow head
floats under to be like snow again.
Then I like to be a woman like the one,
to be with a long wing.

The Stone and I
BY BEVERLY OPSE

On my table lies a stone.
On the stone lies a glass of water.
The water is black with dirt.
The dirt is dry and dusty.
I'd invite a cabbage to eat.
The cabbage is very pleased.
It likes the rock
because it doesn't move.

Everybody
  by Shirley Nielson

I was wearing a blue
coat. It was cabbage and wieners.
They were big cooked wieners,
the smell was cabbage
ah delicious smell
of cabbage out not summer noise was
running water in the kitchen somewhere.

Nervously Sipping Wine

RUSSELL EDSON READ at the University of Minnesota several years ago. He said that he sits down at his typewriter and writes about ten different short pieces at one session. He then comes back later to reread them. Maybe one out of the ten is successful and he keeps that one. He said that if a good first line comes to him, the rest of the piece usually works. Here are some of his first lines:[6]

"A man wants an aeroplane to like him."

"A rat wanted to put its tail in an old woman's vagina. . . ."

"If a scientist had bred pigeons the size of horses . . ."

"A beloved duck gets cooked by mistake."

"A man having to do with an éclair heard his mother breaking something, and figured it must be his father."

"A husband and wife discover that their children are fakes."

"Identical twin old men take turns at being alive."

Here are two complete pieces:

Sautéing

As a man sautéed his hat he was thinking of how his mother used to sauté his father's hat, and how grandmother used to sauté grandfather's hat.

Some garlic and wine and it doesn't taste like hat at all, it tastes like underwear. . . .

And as he sautéed his hat he thought of his mother sautéing his father's hat, and grandmother sautéing grandfather's hat, and wished he had somehow gotten married so he'd have someone to sauté his hat; sautéing is such a lonely thing. . . .

With Sincerest Regrets

Like a white snail the toilet slides into the living room, demanding to be loved.

It is impossible, and we tender our sincerest regrets.

In the book of the heart there is no mention made of plumbing.

And though we have spent our intimacy many times with you, you belong to an unfortunate reference, which we would rather not embrace. . . .

The toilet slides out of the living room like a white snail, flushing with grief. . . .

After the reading, there was the usual wine-and-cheese reception in an ugly, large classroom. I clearly remember Russell Edson in a suit sitting alone across the room. All the students, faculty, and poets stood around the crackers and thin orange cheese slices at the opposite end of the room nervously sipping wine and discussing his work. Few of us approached him. Though we all laughed during the reading, he touched on naked truths in us all and we were uncomfortable.

Try sitting at your typewriter and without thinking begin to write Russell Edson–type pieces. This means letting go and allowing the elm in your front yard to pick itself up and walk over to Iowa. Try for good, strong first sentences. You might want to take the first half of your sentence from a newspaper article and finish the sentence with an ingredient listed in a cookbook. Play around. Dive into absurdity and write. Take chances. You will succeed if you are fearless of failure.

Don't Tell, but Show

THERE'S AN OLD adage in writing: "Don't tell, but show." What does this actually mean? It means don't tell us about anger (or any of those big words like honesty, truth, hate, love, sorrow, life, justice, etc.); show us what made you angry. We will read it and feel angry. Don't tell readers what to feel. Show them the situation, and that feeling will awaken in them.

Writing is not psychology. We do not talk "about" feelings. Instead the writer feels and through her words awakens those feelings in the reader. The writer takes the reader's hand and guides him through the valley of sorrow and joy without ever having to mention those words.

When you are present at the birth of a child you may find yourself weeping and singing. Describe what you see: the mother's face, the rush of energy when the baby finally enters the world after many attempts, the husband breathing with his wife, applying a wet washcloth to her forehead. The reader will understand without your ever having to discuss the nature of life.

When you write, stay in direct connection with the senses and what you are writing about. If you are writing from first thoughts—the way your mind first flashes on something before second and third thoughts take over and comment, criticize, and evaluate—you don't have to worry. First thoughts are the mind reflecting experiences—as close as a human being can get in words to the sunset, the birth, the bobby pin, the crocus. We can't always stay with first thoughts, but it is good to know about them. They can easily teach us how to step out of the way and use words like a mirror to reflect the pictures.

As soon as I hear the word *about* in someone's writing, it is an automatic alarm. "This story is about life." Skip that line and go willy-nilly right into life in your writing. Naturally, when we do practice writing in our notebooks, we might write a general line: "I want to write about my grandmother" or "This is a story about success." That's fine. Don't castigate yourself for writing it; don't get critical and mix up the creator and editor. Simply write it, note it, and drop to a deeper level and enter the story and take us into it.

Some general statements are sometimes very appropriate. Just make sure to back each one with a concrete picture. Even if you are writing an essay, it makes the work so much more lively. Oh, if only Kant or Descartes had followed these instructions. "I think, therefore I am"—I think about bubble gum, horse racing, barbecue, and the stock market; therefore, I know I exist in America in the twentieth century. Go ahead, take Kant's *Prolegomena to Any Future*

Metaphysic and get it to show what he is telling. We would all be a lot happier.

   Several years ago I wrote down a story that someone had told me. My friends said it was boring. I couldn't understand their reaction; I loved the story. What I realize now is that I wrote "about" the story, second-hand. I didn't enter it and make friends with it. I was outside it; therefore, I couldn't take anyone else into it. This does not mean you can't write about something you did not actually experience firsthand; only make sure that you breathe life into it. Otherwise it is two times removed and you are not present.

Be Specific

B E SPECIFIC. Don't say "fruit." Tell what kind of fruit—"It is a pomegranate." Give things the dignity of their names. Just as with human beings, it is rude to say, "Hey, girl, get in line." That "girl" has a name. (As a matter of fact, if she's at least twenty years old, she's a woman, not a "girl" at all.) Things, too, have names. It is much better to say "the geranium in the window" than "the flower in the window." "Geranium"—that one word gives us a much more specific picture. It penetrates more deeply into the beingness of that flower. It immediately gives us the scene by the window—red petals, green circular leaves, all straining toward sunlight.

About ten years ago I decided I had to learn the names of plants and flowers in my environment. I bought a book on them and walked down the tree-lined streets of Boulder, examining leaf, bark, and seed, trying to match them up with their descriptions and names in the book. Maple, elm, oak, locust. I usually tried to cheat by asking people working in their yards the names of the flowers and trees growing there. I was amazed how few people had any idea of the names of the live beings inhabiting their little plot of land.

When we know the name of something, it brings us closer to the ground. It takes the blur out of our mind; it connects us to the earth. If I walk down the street and see "dogwood," "forsythia," I feel more friendly toward the environment. I am noticing what is around me and can name it. It makes me more awake.

If you read the poems of William Carlos Williams, you will see how specific he is about plants, trees, flowers—chicory, daisy, locust, poplar, quince, primrose, black-eyed Susan, lilacs—each has its own integrity. Williams says, "Write what's in front of your nose." It's good for us to know what is in front of our nose. Not just "daisy," but how the flower is in the season we are looking at it—"The dayseye hugging the earth /in August . . . brownedged, /green and pointed scales /armor his yellow."[7] Continue to hone your awareness: to the name, to the month, to the day, and finally to the moment.

Williams also says: "No idea, but in things." Study what is "in front of your nose." By saying "geranium" instead of "flower," you are penetrating more deeply into the present and being there. The closer we can get to what's in front of our nose, the more it can teach us everything. "To see the World in a Grain of Sand, and a heaven in a Wild Flower . . ."[8]

In writing groups and classes too, it is good to

quickly learn the names of all the other group members. It helps to ground you in the group and make you more attentive to each other's work.

Learn the names of everything: birds, cheese, tractors, cars, buildings. A writer is all at once everything—an architect, French cook, farmer—and at the same time, a writer is none of these things.

Big Concentration

OKAY. TAKE SOMETHING specific to write about. Let's say the experience of carving your first spoon out of cedar. Tell us all the details. Penetrate that experience, but at the same time don't become myopic. As you become single-minded in your writing, at the same time something in you should remain aware of the color of the sky or the sound of a distant mower. Just throw in even one line about the street outside your window at the time you were carving that spoon. It is good practice.

We shouldn't forget that the universe moves with us, is at our back with everything we do. And if you throw a line in about it, it reminds the reader, too, that though we must concentrate on the task before us, we mustn't forget the whole breathing world. Tossing in the color of the sky at the right moment lets the piece breathe a little more.

If you are on a Zen meditation retreat, between forty-minute sittings you do kinhin, walking zazen. Very, very slowly, in a standing position, in coordination with your out-breath, you begin the motion of taking a step. You can feel both knees slightly bend, your heel lift off the floor. Very slow. On the in-breath, you actually lift the ball and toes of the foot and step forward about one inch. Then you repeat the process with the other foot. Kinhin lasts about ten minutes. In the act of slowing down that much, you realize you don't take isolated individual steps. With every step you take, you feel the air, the windows, the other meditators. You become aware that there would be no step without the floor, the sky, the water you drink to stay alive. Everything is interconnected, interpenetrated. Even the season we step in supports our step.

So when we concentrate in our writing, it is good. But we should always concentrate, not by blocking out the world, but by allowing it all to exist. This is a very tricky balance.

The Ordinary
and Extraordinary

I WAS CAMPING this weekend in Abiquiu among fantastic pink cliffs and bare hills. It is the place that Georgia O'Keeffe chose to live. The weekend before that, I was in Hopi land in Arizona to see the snake dances. There were complete moonscapes that you could look out over from atop First and Second Mesa. The snake dances were for rain. Snakes were caught, all kinds—bullheads, rattlers, blue racers—and medicine men sat with them for four days and nights before the dance. During the dance the men of the village put them between their teeth and moved rhythmically back and forth. When the dance was completed, the dancers ran down the long mesa with the snakes and let them go in all four directions, the same directions where they had collected them.

I looked and looked in wonder. "How could I ever write about these vast expanses and mythic rituals?" A friend who had been with me asked: "Look at this huge space, the hills and mesas and the sky. You can feel God here. How can you just use the original detail that you talk about to capture this?"

We mistake detail for being picayune or only for

writing about ants and bobby pins. We think of detail as small, not the realm of the cosmic mind or these big hills of New Mexico. That isn't true. No matter how large a thing is, how fantastic, it is also ordinary. We think of details as daily and mundane. Even miracles are mundane happenings that an awakened mind can see in a fantastic way.

So it is not merely a materialistic handling of objects that is the base for writing, but using details to step through to the other shore—to the vast emptiness behind it all. For the Hopi Indians, who had always lived there, the large expanses around their village were very ordinary. They saw the huge mesas every day. Unfortunately, many of the young people want to leave to go to the city where it is more exciting.

Original details are very ordinary, except to the mind that sees their extraordinariness. It's not that we need to go to the Hopi mesas to see greatness; we need to view what we already have in a different way. It is very deep for the Hopis to have a snake dance, but it also is one of their festivals that has been performed every other year for their whole lives. Like any other dance, when it was over, they invited friends to their homes for dinner. If we see their lives and festivals as fantastic and our lives as ordinary, we come to writing with a sense of poverty. We must remember that everything is ordinary and extraordinary. It is our minds that either open or close. Details are not good or bad. They are details. How do you get to First

Mesa? Go west one and a half hours from Window Rock on Highway 264.

The snake dance was made up of detail after detail with extreme concentration; it had to be that way—the snakes were in the Hopis' mouths. We who watched thought it was unfathomable and fantastic because it was new and foreign. It was also ordinary and had been done for hundreds of years. In order to write about it, we have to go to the heart of it and know it, so the ordinary and extraordinary flash before our eyes simultaneously. Go so deep into something that you understand its interpenetration with all things. Then automatically the detail is imbued with the cosmic; they are interchangeable.

A friend of mine had a motorcycle accident recently. He had not slept the night before and left early for a long journey to Massachusetts. He fell asleep at eighty-five miles per hour and ran into a car. He was very lucky and didn't have a scratch on him, though his bike was totaled.

I was shattered when I heard about it. If he had been killed, the balance of my life would have changed. We are all interwoven and create each other's universes. When one person dies out of his time, it affects us all. We don't live for ourselves; we are interconnected. We live for the earth, for Texas, for the chicken we ate last night that gave us its life, for our mother, for the highway and the ceiling and the trees. We have a responsibility to treat ourselves kindly; then we will treat the world in the same way.

This understanding is how we should come to writing. Then we can handle details not as individual, material objects alone but as reflections of everything. Katagiri Roshi said: "It is very deep to have a cup of tea." Understand that when we write about a cup or a mesa or the sky or a bobby pin, we must give them good attention and penetrate into their heart. Doing this, we will naturally make those leaps that poetry talks about, because we are aware of the interconnection of all things. We can also write prose that moves from paragraph to paragraph without having to worry about those transitions we were taught about in high school. They will happen naturally, because we will be in touch with the hugeness of movement.

Talk Is the Exercise Ground

G ET TOGETHER WITH a good friend and tell stories. Tell about the time you had your palm
read in Albuquerque, how you sat zazen in a chicken
coop in Arroyo Seco, New Mexico, with your friend
Sassafras, how your mother eats cottage cheese and
toast every morning.

When you tell friends stories, you want them to
listen, so you make the stories colorful; you might ex-
aggerate, even add a few brilliant white lies. And your
friends don't care if it's all not precisely as it was ten
years ago; it is now and they are entranced. A writing
friend once said to me when I met him for lunch:
"Tell me the best piece of gossip you heard in the last
month. And if you don't know any, make it up." Grace
Paley, a New York short story writer, said, "It is the
responsibility of writers to listen to gossip and pass it
on. It is the way all storytellers learn about life."

It is good to talk. Do not be ashamed of it. Talk is
the exercise ground for writing. It is a way we learn
about communication—what makes people interested, what makes them bored. I laugh with friends
and say, "We are not gossiping cruelly. We are just
trying to understand life." And it is true. We should

learn to talk, not with judgment, greed, or envy, but with compassion, wonder, and amazement.

I remember sitting after a concert in the New French Bar in downtown Minneapolis with a writing friend and telling her about how I became a Buddhist. Because of the intensity of her listening, the story, which I had told many times, took on a great brilliance. I remember the light off the wineglasses, the taste of my chocolate mousse. I knew then that I had to write the story—there was great material in it.

Talk is a way writers can help each other find new directions. "Hey, that's great; have you written about it?" "That's a good line, 'I lived here six years and can't remember a thing, not a thing.' Write it down and begin a poem with it." Once I came home from a visit in Boston and said to a friend in passing, "Oh, he's crazy about her." She was in the process of writing a mystery novel in those days and honed in, "How can you tell he was crazy about her? Tell me what actions he did." I laughed. You can't make general statements around writers—they want me not to "tell" but to "show" with incidents.

Another friend told me about her father who left the family suddenly when she was twelve and became a born-again Christian and embezzled money from the churches of three states. It was her personal tragedy. I told her it was a great story. Her face lit up. She realized she could transform her life in a new way—as material for writing.

Talk is a way to warm up for the big game—the hours you write alone with your pen and notebook. Make a list of all the stories you have told over and over. That's a lot of writing to be done.

Writing Is a Communal Act

Astudent said, "I'm reading so much Heming-way, I'm afraid I'm beginning to sound like him. I'm copying him and not having my own voice." That's not so bad. It's a lot better to sound like Ernest Hemingway than like Aunt Bethune, who thinks Hallmark greeting cards contain the best poetry in America.

We always worry that we are copying someone else, that we don't have our own style. Don't worry. Writing is a communal act. Contrary to popular belief, a writer is not Prometheus alone on a hill full of fire. We are very arrogant to think we alone have a totally original mind. We are carried on the backs of all the writers who came before us. We live in the present with all the history, ideas, and soda pop of this time. It all gets mixed up in our writing.

Writers are great lovers. They fall in love with other writers. That's how they learn to write. They take on a writer, read everything by him or her, read it over again until they understand how the writer moves, pauses, and sees. That's what being a lover is: stepping out of yourself, stepping into someone else's skin. Your ability to love another's writing means those capabilities are awakened in you. It will only make you bigger; it won't make you a copy cat. The parts of another's writing that are natural to you will become you, and you will use some of those moves when you write. But not artificially. Great lovers realize that they are what they are in love with. That is what happened to Allen Ginsberg when he wanted to write so that Jack Kerouac could understand him: ". . . being in love with Jack Kerouac he discovered he was Jack Kerouac: that's something love knows."[9] You are Ernest Hemingway on a safari when you read *Green Hills of Africa,* and then you are Jane Austen looking at Regency women and then Gertrude Stein doing her own Cubism in words, and then you are Larry McMurtry in Texas walking to the pool hall in a dusty town.

So writing is not just writing. It is also having a relationship with other writers. And don't be jealous, especially secretly. That's the worst kind. If someone writes something great, it's just more clarity in the world for all of us. Don't make writers "other," different from you: "They are good and I am bad." Don't create that dichotomy. It makes it hard to become good if you create that duality. The opposite, of course, is also true: if you say, "I am great and they aren't," then you become too proud, unable to grow as a writer or hear criticism of your work. Just: "They are good and I am good." That statement gives a lot of space. "They have been at it longer, and I can walk their path for a while and learn from them."

It's much better to be a tribal writer, writing for all people and reflecting many voices through us, than to be a cloistered being trying to find one peanut of truth in our own individual mind. Become big and write with the whole world in your arms.

Even if we go off alone to write in the wilderness, we have to commune with ourselves and everything around us: the desk, the trees, the birds, the water, the typewriter. We are not separate from everything else. It's only our egos that make us think we are. We build on what came before us, even if our writing is a reaction to it or we try to negate the past. We still write with the knowledge of what's at our backs.

It's also good to know some local people who are writing and whom you can get together with for mutual support. It is very hard to continue just on your own. I tell my students in a group to get to know each other, to share their work with other people. Don't let it just pile up in notebooks. Let it out. Kill the idea of the lone, suffering artist. We suffer anyway as human beings. Don't make it any harder on yourself.

One Plus One Equals
a Mercedes-Benz

I ALWAYS TELL my students, especially the sixth-graders, the ones who are becoming very worldly-wise: Turn off your logical brain that says 1 + 1 = 2. Open up your mind to the possibility that 1 + 1 can equal 48, a Mercedes-Benz, an apple pie, a blue horse. Don't tell your autobiography with facts, such as "I am in sixth grade. I am a boy. I live in Owatonna. I have a mother and father." Tell me who you really are: "I am the frost on the window, the cry of a young wolf, the thin blade of grass."

Forget yourself. Disappear into everything you look at—a street, a glass of water, a cornfield. Everything you feel, become totally that feeling, burn all of yourself with it. Don't worry—your ego will quickly become nervous and stop such ecstasy. But if you can catch that feeling or smell or sight the moment you are one with it, you probably will have a great poem.

Then we fall back on the earth again. Only the writing stays with the great vision. That's why we have to go back again and again to books—good books, that is. And read again and again the visions of who we are, how we can be. The struggle we go through as human beings, so we can again and again have compassion for ourselves and treat each other kindly.

Be an Animal

WHEN YOU ARE not writing, you are a writer too. It doesn't leave you. Walk with an animal walk and take in everything around you as prey. Use your senses as an animal does. Watch a cat when he sees something moving in the room. He is perfectly still, and at the same time, his every sense is alive, watching, listening, smelling. This is how you should be when you are in the streets. The cat's mind is not thinking about how much money he needs, or whom to write a post-card to when he visits Florence: he is watching the mouse or the marble rolling across the floor or the light reflecting in crystal. He is ready with all of him to pounce. Now, you don't have to get down on all fours and twitch your tail. Only be still—some part of you, at least—and know where you are, no matter how busy you are.

My friend who went with me to Europe had a phobia about getting lost. She'd never learned to read a city map or pick up simple signals, like "We were in this piazza yesterday. There, across the street, is the Savoy Hotel, where we bought concert tickets, so that must be the turn." Because she was scared, she lost all touch with her common sense, with the natural senses that we rely on as our survival tools. That place in us that is aware and that is always awake. Katagiri Roshi said: "You are Buddha right now!" Only we forget when we are busy or frightened, as my friend was. Afraid of being lost, she became lost.

As writers we have to walk in the world in touch with that present, alert part of ourselves, that animal sense part that looks, sees, and notices—street signs, corners, fire hydrants, newspaper stands.

Also, right before you are planning to write, a good preparation is to become an animal. Move slowly, stalking your prey, which is whatever you plan to write about, no matter what else you might be doing at the moment—taking out the garbage, walking to the library, watering the garden. Get all your senses intent. Turn off your logical mind—empty, no thoughts. Let your words come from your belly. Bring your brain down to your stomach and digest your thoughts. Let them give nourishment to your body. Have a round belly, like Buddha, breathing all the way inside. Don't hold in your stomach. Be patient and measured. Let the writing percolate below the level of thought forms, in the subconscious and through your veins.

Then, when you finally pounce, let's say at ten A.M., your designated time to write that day, add the pressure of timed writing. Write for an hour, or twenty minutes, whatever amount you decide, but write for all it's worth. Keep your hand moving, pour out everything, straight from your veins, through your pen and onto paper. Don't stop. Don't doodle. Don't daydream. Write until you're spent.

But don't worry. This isn't your last chance. If you missed the mouse today, you'll get it tomorrow. You never leave who you are. If you are a writer when writing, you also are a writer when you are cooking, sleeping, walking. And if you are a mother, a painter, a horse, a giraffe, or a carpenter, you will bring that into your writing, too. It comes with you. You can't divorce yourself from parts of yourself.

Best come to writing whole with everything in you. And when you're done writing, best to walk out in the street with everything you are, including your common sense or Buddha nature—something good at the center, to tell you the names of streets, so you won't get lost. Something to tell you you can come back to your writing tomorrow and stay with your writing in the hours in between, when you are an animal, out stalking the city.

Make Statements
and Answer Questions

I N THE EARLY seventies there was a study done on women and language that affected me very deeply and also affected my writing. One of the things the study said was that women add on qualifiers to their statements. For instance, "The Vietnam war is awful, isn't it?" "I like this, don't you?" In their sentence structure women were always looking for reinforcement for their feelings and opinions. They didn't just make statements and stand behind them: "This is beautiful." "This is terrible." They needed encouragement from outside themselves. (By the way, what they found to be true for women they also mentioned was true for minorities.)

Another thing women did in their speech was to use a lot of words like *perhaps, maybe, somehow.* Indefinite modifiers. For instance, "Somehow it happened." As though the force were beyond understanding and left the woman powerless. "Maybe I'll go." Again, not a clear assertive statement like "Yes, I'll go."

The world isn't always black and white. A person may not be sure if she can go some place, but it is important, especially for a beginning writer, to make clear, assertive statements. "This is good." "It was a blue horse." Not "Well, I know it sounds funny, but I think perhaps it was a blue horse." Making statements is practice in trusting your own mind, in learning to stand up with your thoughts.

After I read the article, I went home and looked at a poem I had just written. I made myself take out all vague, indefinite words and phrases. It felt as though I were pulling towels off my body, and I was left standing naked after a shower, exposing who I really was and how I felt. It was scary the first time, but it felt good. It made the poem much better.

So even though life is not always so clear, it is good to express yourself in clear, affirmative statements. "This is how I think and feel." "This is who I am in this moment." It takes practice, but it is very rewarding.

But while you are practicing writing, do not worry if you see yourself using those indefinite words. Don't condemn yourself or be critical. Just be aware of it. Keep writing. When you go back over it, you can cut them out.

Another thing you should watch out for are questions. If you can write a question, you can answer it. When you are writing, if you write a question, that is fine. But immediately go to a deeper level inside yourself and answer it in the next line. "What should I do with my life?" I should eat three brownies, remember the sky, and become the best writer in the world. "Why did I feel weird last night?" Because I ate pigeon for dinner and I wore my shoes on the wrong feet and because I am unhappy. "Where does the wind come from?" It comes from the memory of pioneers on the Croix River. It loves the earth as far as the Dakotas.

Don't be afraid to answer the questions. You will find endless resources inside yourself. Writing is the act of burning through the fog in your mind. Don't carry the fog out on paper. Even if you are not sure of something, express it as though you know yourself. With this practice you eventually will.

The Action of a Sentence

VERBS ARE VERY important. They are the action and energy of a sentence. Be aware of how you use them. Try this exercise. Fold a sheet of paper in half the long way. On the left side of the page list ten nouns. Any ten.

> lilacs
> horse
> mustache
> cat
> fiddle
> muscles
> dinosaur
> seed
> plug
> video

Now turn the paper over to the right column. Think of an occupation; for example, a carpenter, doctor, flight attendant. List fifteen verbs on the right half of the page that go with that position.

A Cook:
sauté
chop
mince
slice
cut
heat
broil
taste
boil
bake
fry
marinate
whip
stir
scoop

Open the page. You have nouns listed in a row down the left side and verbs listed on the right. Try joining the nouns with the verbs to see what new combinations you can get, and then finish the sentences, casting the verbs in the past tense if you need to.

	A Cook:
lilacs	sauté
horse	chop
mustache	mince
cat	slice

fiddle	cut
muscles	heat
dinosaur	broil
seed	taste
plug	boil
video	bake
	fry
	marinate
	whip
	stir
	scoop

Dinosaurs marinate in the earth.
The fiddles boiled the air with their music.
The lilacs sliced the sky into purple.

Here are some other examples of the use of verbs:

Her husband's breath *sawing* her sleep in half . . .
The sunken light of late day *stretches* on their pro-
    pane tank.[10]

I *exploded* when I saw him . . .[11]
Others in pairs in cars to the moon *flashing* river.[12]

. . . where angels and gladiolas *walk* your skin / to
    sleep in the earth . . .[13]

My blood *buzzes* like a hornet's nest.[14]

This does not mean that while you are writing you should stop and contemplate a new verb for an hour. Only, be aware of your verbs and the power they have and use them in fresh ways. The more you are awake to all aspects of language, the more vibrant your writing will be. You might decide ultimately that *run, see, go,* are for you. That's fine, but then it is a choice you make rather than some place in your sentence where you are unaware, asleep and snoring.

Writing in Restaurants

I AM SITTING in a dining car in San Cristóbal, New Mexico. The town has about sixty-eight people, and the Spanish woman who runs the diner has owned the land since 1948. She just returned from Arizona and has opened it again. The town says she has to dig her own well, so until she does there is no cooking on the premises. Therefore, my choices for this two-hour writing session are cigarettes, Coke, Mountain Dew, Tom's Red Twists, Super Bubble in plain, grape, or apple, Snickers, Fire Stix, Alka-Seltzer, Tums, Kool-Aid in raspberry or tropical punch flavor, a quart of milk, or a dozen eggs. I must order something and it must be more than a Coke, because I hope to be here awhile.

That is the first rule. When you select a café to write in, you must establish a relationship. Go hungry so you will want to eat. There have been times when I wasn't hungry and ordered a meal anyway, then pushed it aside and took out my notebook. Occasionally, I picked at the fried onions or the spinach salad during the next hour or so. If I order coffee, I don't take advantage of the free refills. I want the people in the restaurant to know I appreciate the time and space they are giving me. Also, if you are taking up a table for a few hours, leave more than the ordinary tip. The waitress makes money on table turnover, and you are staying longer than your turn. Do not show up at lunch or dinner when they are the most crowded. Go at the end of rush hour when the waitress will be glad to see you, because she is very tired and knows you won't order a lot and don't expect fast service.

I know this sounds like a very expensive way to write, but this is only the first time. After the initial introduction, you begin quite easily to become a routine. "Oh, there's the writer. How's it going? Want a coffee refill on the house?"

When I lived in Minneapolis, a friend called and said, "A new restaurant just opened at Calhoun Square. Let's have dinner and write there." That's when I first realized that there is an art to selecting a good writing place. This new restaurant was totally inappropriate; I could tell at first glance. First of all, it was too fancy and was bent on serving good, creative dishes. They wanted people eating. They didn't want great literature written while we leaned on their violet, pale blue, and white linen tablecloths.

Usually, I pick original places, not chain restaurants like McDonald's. Besides the fact that chain restaurants are all plastic, the seats are often uncomfortable. You want a place that lends a human atmosphere, not everything efficient, stiff, and bright orange.

But why go to all this bother? Why not just stay

home and write? It is a trick I use. It's good to change the scenery from time to time, and at home there is the telephone, the refrigerator, the dishes to be washed, a shower to be taken, the letter carrier to greet. It's good to get away. Also, if you made the effort to get to a café, you can't leave so quickly to do something else the way you can in your own home.

And the mind is a trickster. It seems that when I write, a hundred pleasurable activities come to mind that I would rather do. I remember once being given a cabin in northern Minnesota for a week. The second day I was sitting down in front of the typewriter to work on a short story. There was a view of late June aspens and beet leaves, lettuce, zinnias from the garden. A great blue sky. Suddenly I was in a bathing suit, ankle-deep in the lake, which was a quarter of a mile from the cabin. About to dive headfirst, I became awake: "Natalie, what are you doing here? You just sat down to write the third page of your short story!" Usually I don't get quite that far before I catch myself.

We can give it different names, but basically it is that part of our mind that is resistant that begins to activate when we do these tricks. What does it want to resist? Work and concentration.

There was a period last fall when every time I began to write, I went into a perfect blank-minded euphoria, where I stared out the window and felt a love for and oneness with everything. I sat in this state, sometimes for the whole time I had planned to write. I thought to myself, "Lo and behold, I am becoming enlightened! This is much more important than writing, and besides this is where all writing leads." After this had gone on for quite a while, I asked Katagiri Roshi about it. He said, "Oh, it's just laziness. Get to work."

I have read about flotation tanks, where sensory input is reduced considerably, since you are in a dark box, immersed in ten inches of warm water. Concentration is increased because of the restriction of sensory stimulation.

Oddly enough, writing in a café can work, too, to improve concentration. But instead of reducing stimulation, the café atmosphere keeps that sensory part of you busy and happy, so that the deeper, quieter part of you that creates and concentrates is free to do so. It is something like occupying a baby with tricks, while slipping the spoon full of applesauce into her mouth. Mozart used to have his wife read stories to him while he was composing for the same reason.

The stimulation in a restaurant can also be used in another way. Turn to face it and get on that carousel and go for a ride. Keeping your hand moving, write with the waves of energy, throwing in details you catch from around you and mixing them with your own thought flashes. The outside excitement can stimulate and awaken feelings inside you. There is a wonderful give and take.

In Paris, I was astounded by how many cafés there

were. It is considered impolite to hurry a customer. You can order one coffee at eight A.M. and still be sipping it with no pressure at three P.M. Hemingway in *A Moveable Feast* (it's a great book!—read it!) tells of writing in cafés in Paris and how James Joyce might be a few tables away. When I arrived there last June, I understood why so many American writers became expatriates: there are probably five cafés to every block in Paris, and they are all beckoning you to write, and writing in them is very acceptable.

In America, people are wary of writing. Except for filling out a form or writing a check, they think it is very exotic, so they leave you alone, though some are secretly fascinated and glance over at you every once in a while. Writing is not a natural part of the American context. Use that attitude to your advantage. You will be left alone when you write in public. Only once, when I was in Nebraska, did a warm, friendly waitress come over and address it directly: "What are you writing about? Can I read it?" If I hadn't been on the road and in a rush, I would have gladly sat her down with my last forty pages.

Oh, yes, in the Rainbow Café, a 3.2 bar in Hill City, Minnesota, a teenager playing pool one afternoon, as I was writing at a nearby booth, yelled over to me, "Hey, you write faster than I think." And a little later, "If you keep this up and come back tomorrow, the whole town'll be out here to watch you." Always laugh, respond, stay friendly.

Make a list of cafés, restaurants, and bars you've been in. Add details, if you want. See where it leads. Be specific.

Terry's Cafe in South Dakota, where I wrote postcards to my friends in Minnesota. "Dear Phil: I'm in South Dakota. I'm heading for New Mexico. It is late July. Know I love your cabin by the St. Croix. Remember me. Forgive me for leaving. I am eating a salad with canned beans and saltine crackers."

Costa's Coffee Shop in Owatonna, Minnesota, across from the Louis Sullivan Bank. The orange booths and the Greek salads with too much oil.

Snyder's Drugstore, where Jim told me he loved the ham sandwiches. . . .

Also, please note: don't forget to try writing in laundromats.

The Writing Studio

IF YOU WANT a room to write in, just get a room. Don't make a big production out of it. If it doesn't leak, has a window, heat in the winter, then put in your desk, bookshelves, a soft chair, and start writing. Too many people decide they have to paint the walls, then buy wall hangings, a special desk, reupholster a chair, hire a carpenter to build walnut bookshelves, shop for a superb rug. "After all, this is my special room."

It becomes another trick to avoid writing. I have watched friends who made perfect spaces and then couldn't bear to go into them. They felt more comfortable writing at the kitchen table. It's hard to sit in an exquisite space and rub against our imperfections which writing brings up. We make these exquisite rooms of silence and then long to write in noisy, chaotic cafés. Many of us make beautiful, orderly gardens in the summer and then wish we were in the woods where there are fallen trees, bugs, and apparent wild disorder. It is natural in our studios to have books lying open, at least one cup half filled with old black tea, papers spread out, piles of unanswered letters, a graham cracker box, shoes kicked under the desk, a watch with a broken second hand lying on the floor.

Zen teachers talk about our rooms as an indication of our state of mind. Some people are afraid of space and so fill every nook and cranny. It is analogous to our mind's fear of emptiness, so the mind constantly stirs up thoughts and dramas. But I think it is different with a writing space. A little apparent disorder is an indication of the fertility of the mind and some-one that is actively creating. A perfect studio has always told me that the person is afraid of his own mind and is reflecting in his outward space an inward need for control. Creativity is just the opposite: it is a loss of control.

It is good to give ourselves a writing room and a place to put our writing tools, but we should know ourselves well enough not to become lost in interior decoration. I remember the first studio I rented for seventy-five dollars a month. It was a big room on the third floor of someone else's house. It had unfinished floors and three windows. With the owners at home, I had to befriend a Doberman pinscher for three days before the dog would let me in the house when no one else was there. But even with that, it was very important for me to have a place all my own to write in and in another part of the city. It meant I took myself seriously. A year before that I had agonized over spending forty-six dollars for a tape recorder to practice reading poetry aloud, and I would never think of spending the money for an electric type-writer. As I developed and my commitment grew, I was more willing to spend money for writing. Creating a writing space is another indication of your increased commitment.

Please note, though, that just last week I met Meridel le Sueur in Taos, New Mexico. She is a writer in her eighties who has written several novels, short stories, poetry books. She said she lives nowhere now. She visits people, stays in their homes, and writes wherever she is. She just came from California, where she visited her daughter, and was now going to stay with friends in Taos and write there. She asked if there was a place she could purchase an old manual typewriter for about thirty dollars. After she finishes with it, she'll give it away, as she does in each place she visits, so she doesn't have to lug it with her to her next destination. So much for writing studios!

A Big Topic: Eroticism

You might have some large topic that you really feel the need to write about, for example, "Love and Eroticism." With a big topic such as this, there is always the chance of becoming philosophical and abstract and usually long-winded, boring, and never getting closer to what you need to say. "Ah, yes, eroticism. I believe it has to do with sexual instincts and behavior. . . ." Underneath, while you write you are a little nervous, not knowing how to get to what you really need to say and also a little afraid to get there. Relax.

Always begin with yourself and let that carry you. *Eroticism* is a big word. If you are nervous, look around the room. Begin with something small and concrete—your teacup in its saucer, the thin slice of an apple, an Oreo cookie crumb on your red lips. Sometimes you have to begin far away from the answer and then down-spiral back to it. Writing is the act of discovery. You want to discover your relationship with a topic, not the dictionary definition.

"Where do I come from?"—a student in New Mexico addressed this in a timed-writing exercise. She began by writing about something that had just happened—visiting a friend in the maternity ward.

She wrote the details of the visit and how she made the husband, wife, and new infant a Thanksgiving dinner. All the while you felt her humming with the original question. In the middle of the turkey dinner in Santa Fe she switched to Brooklyn, her birth, and her mother. You can't always attack a topic; sometimes it takes a while to come to it.

Katagiri Roshi said about couples, "You should walk side by side, not face to face." That is how we should approach what we need to say: not head-on and aggressively, but with a little side dance. If you feel erotic and write about eating a melon, though you never mention the word, we will read it and feel erotic too.

But do not think this means you can't become brazen if that's what you need to say about eroticism. Only, if you remove your clothes immediately and plunge into the water, it may be too cold. You'll jump out again, saying, "It's too big a task." Approach eroticism from across the shore, fully clothed, and take your time swimming across the river. If you start taking off your shirt and pants slowly as you swim, by the time you get to the other side you'll be naked— brazenly erotic, the way you always wanted to be, but you won't be so frightened or embarrassed by it. You took your time getting there; you are on the solid ground of the other shore and we did the crawl along with you. We're willing to listen to anything you have to say. Now go ahead, get wild.

Also, you might try to approach a big topic from another angle. Break the topic down into its different aspects. If the word *eroticism* makes you balk or leaves you tongue-tied, make it more intriguing. Try these:

What makes you hot?
List all the sexual fruits you know.
What do you eat when you're not in love?
What part of your body is the most erotic?
"The body becomes the landscape."—Meridel le Sueur
What do you connect with?
The very first time you felt erotic.

If you don't know what erotic is, write as though you do. Okay. You have ten minutes. Choose one of the above and write. Remember to be specific. Go. Keep your hand moving. Don't edit.

A Tourist in Your Own Town

W RITERS WRITE ABOUT things that other people don't pay much attention to. For instance, our tongues, elbows, water coming out of a water faucet, the kind of garbage trucks New York City has, the color purple of a faded sign in a small town. I always tell my elementary school students, "Please, no more Michael Jacksons, Atari games, TV characters in your poems." They get all the attention they need, plus millions of dollars in advertising to ensure their popularity. A writer's job is to make the ordinary come alive, to awaken ourselves to the specialness of simply being.

When we live in a place for too long, we grow dull. We don't notice what is around us. That is why a trip is so exciting. We are in a new place and see everything in a fresh way. I have a friend who lives in New York. The last time she'd been to the Empire State Building was in fifth grade when her public school took her there. When friends came to visit from Minnesota, of course, they wanted to go to that great skyscraper. She was thrilled to go to the top again, though she would never have done it on her own or cared about it.

A writer is a visitor from the Midwest to New York City for the first time, only she never leaves the Midwest; she sees her own town with the eyes of a tourist in New York City. And she begins to see her life this way too. Recently I moved to Santa Fe, and since there were few writing jobs here, I worked as a cook part-time in a local restaurant. Waking up at six on Sunday to cook brunch all day, I questioned my fate. At eight A.M. I was busy cutting carrots at a diagonal, noticing the orange of them and thinking to myself, "This is really very deep." I fell in love with the carrots. I laughed. "So this is what has become of me! Too easily satisfied with so little."

Learn to write about the ordinary. Give homage to old coffee cups, sparrows, city buses, thin ham sandwiches. Make a list of everything ordinary you can think of. Keep adding to it. Promise yourself, before you leave the earth, to mention everything on your list at least once in a poem, short story, newspaper article.

Write Anyplace

OKAY. YOUR KIDS are climbing into the cereal box. You have $1.25 left in your checking account. Your husband can't find his shoes, your car won't start, you know you have lived a life of unfulfilled dreams. There is the threat of a nuclear holocaust, there is apartheid in South Africa, it is twenty degrees below zero outside, your nose itches, and you don't have even three plates that match to serve dinner on. Your feet are swollen, you need to make a dentist appointment, the dog needs to be let out, you have to defrost the chicken and make a phone call to your cousin in Boston, you're worried about your mother's glaucoma, you forgot to put film in the camera, Safeway has a sale on solid white tuna, you are waiting for a job offer, you just bought a computer and you have to unpack it. You have to start eating sprouts and stop eating doughnuts, you lost your favorite pen, and the cat peed on your current notebook.

Take out another notebook, pick up another pen, and just write, just write, just write. In the middle of the world, make one positive step. In the center of chaos, make one definitive act. Just write. Say yes, stay alive, be awake. Just write. Just write. Just write.

Finally, there is no perfection. If you want to write, you have to cut through and write. There is no perfect atmosphere, notebook, pen, or desk, so train yourself to be flexible. Try writing under different circumstances and in different places. Try trains, buses, at kitchen tables, alone in the woods leaning against a tree, by a stream with your feet in the water, in the desert sitting on a rock, on the curb in front of your house, on a porch, a stoop, in the back seat of a car, in the library, at a lunch counter, in an alley, at the unemployment office, in the dentist's waiting room, at a bar in a wooden booth, at the airport, in Texas, Kansas, or Guatemala, while sipping a Coke, smoking a cigarette, eating a bacon, lettuce, and tomato sandwich.

Recently, I was in New Orleans and went to visit a cemetery where the graves are aboveground because of the water level. I brought my notebook, sat on the cement leaning against the thin shade of a tombstone in the thick heat of Louisiana, and wrote. An hour had passed when I looked up again. I thought to myself, "This is perfect." It wasn't the physical accommodations that were perfect, but when we are in the heart of writing it doesn't matter where we are: it is perfect. There is a great sense of autonomy and security to know we can write anyplace. If you want to write, finally you'll find a way no matter what.

Go Further

PUSH YOURSELF BEYOND when you think you are
done with what you have to say. Go a little further.
Sometimes when you think you are done, it is just the
edge of beginning. Probably that's why we decide we're
done. It's getting too scary. We are touching down onto
something real. It is beyond the point when you think
you are done that often something strong comes out.

I remember one student whose mother had died
of cancer. She would write one side of a page about
it—simple, good prose—and then she would quit.
When she read those pieces in class, I always felt
there was more and told her so. She smiled and said,
"Well, the ten minutes were up." Write to the elev-
enth minute if you need to. I know it can be frighten-
ing and a real loss of control, but I promise you, you
can go through to the other side and actually come
out singing. You might cry a little before the singing,
but that is okay. Just keep your hand moving as you
are feeling. Often, as I write my best pieces, my heart
is breaking.

When I teach writing to young kids, many times
they will write short stories with very complicated
story lines, and instead of pushing themselves to

resolve the story, they use the trick "And then I woke up!" When you continue to stop yourself from going all the way in your writing and coming to a deep resolution, it's not a dream you wake up from, but you carry the nightmare out into the streets. Writing gives you a great opportunity to swim through to freedom.

Even if you *have* pushed yourself and feel you've broken through, push yourself further. If you are on, ride that wave as long as you can. Don't stop in the middle. That moment won't come back exactly in that way again, and it will take much more time trying to finish a piece later on than completing it now.

I give this advice out of pure experience. Go further than you think you can.

Engendering Compassion

I AM ON a Greek island right now: the Aegean Sea, cheap rooms on the beach, nude swimming, little tavernas where you sit under dried bamboo sipping ouzo, taste octopus, watch the great sun set. I am thirty-six and my friend who is with me is thirty-nine. It is the first time either of us has been to Europe. We take in everything, but only halfway because we are busy always, always talking. I tell her about my dance recital when I was six years old in a pink tutu; how my father, who sat in the front row, broke down weeping when he saw me. She tells me how her husband in Catholic school in Nebraska came late for a play that he was the star of and how the nuns had all the school-children on their knees praying that he would appear.

On Tuesday I decide I need to be alone. I want to walk around and write. Everyone has a great fear in life. Mine is loneliness. Naturally our great fear is usually the one most important to overcome to reach our life's dreams. I am a writer. Writers spend a lot of time alone writing. Also, being an artist in our society makes us lonely. Everyone else leaves in the morning for work and structured jobs. Artists live outside that built-in social system.

So I have chosen to spend the day alone because I always want to push my boundaries. It's noon, very hot. I am not going to the beach and everything is closed here at midday. I begin to wonder what I am doing with my life. Whenever I get disoriented or not sure of myself, it seems I bring my whole life into question. It becomes very painful. To cut through, I say to myself, "Natalie, you planned to write. Now write. I don't care if you feel nuts and lonely." So I begin. I write about the nearby church, the boat in the harbor, my table in the café. It isn't great fun. I am wondering when my friend will return. She doesn't come back with the five-o'clock boat.

I can't speak Greek. I am all by myself and notice my environment much more acutely. The four old men at the next table take the long string out of the back of every green bean they have piled on the table. The one facing the ocean argues with the man to his left. An old woman in black near the wharf bends to pull up her long stocking. I wander to a beach I didn't know before and begin reading *Green Hills of Africa* on a sand bar as the sun sets. I notice a taverna that sells fresh tuna. I am attempting to connect with my environment. I miss my friend very much, but through my panic I break through to a kinship with the sand, the sky, my life. I walk back along the beach.

When we walk around Paris, my friend is afraid of being lost and she is very panicky. I don't fear being lost. If I am lost, I am lost. That is all. I look on my map and find my way. I even like to wander the streets of Paris not particularly knowing where I am. In the same way I need to wander in the field of aloneness and learn to enjoy it, and when loneliness bites, take out a map and find my way out without panic, without jumping to the existential nothingness of the world, questioning everything—"Why should I be a writer?"—and pushing myself off the abyss.

So when we write and begin with an empty page and a heart unsure, a famine of thoughts, a fear of no feeling—just begin from there, from that electricity. This kind of writing is uncontrolled, is not sure where the outcome is, and it begins in ignorance and darkness. But facing those things, writing from that place, will eventually break us and open us to the world as it is. Out of this tornado of fear will come a genuine writing voice.

While I was in Paris I read *Tropic of Cancer* by Henry Miller. In the second-to-last chapter Miller rages on about a school in Dijon, France, where he is stuck teaching English, about the dead statues and students who would become dentists and engineers, the cold bone winter and the whole town pumping out mustard. He is furious that he must be there. Then right at the end of the chapter, he sits, late at night, outside the college gates in perfect peace, surrendering himself for the moment to where he is, knowing nothing is good or bad, just alive.

To begin writing from our pain eventually engenders compassion for our small and groping lives. Out of this broken state there comes a tenderness for the cement below our feet, the dried grass cracking in a terrible wind. We can touch the things around us we once thought ugly and see their special detail, the peeling paint and gray of shadows as they are—simply what they are: not bad, just part of the life around us—and love this life because it is ours and in the moment there is nothing better.

Doubt Is Torture

A FRIEND OF MINE was planning to move to Los Angeles with the hope of connecting with the music industry. He was a musician and songwriter, and it was time for him to follow his aspirations. Katagiri Roshi said to him, "Well, if you've really decided to go, let's see what your attitude is."

"Well, I'll try my best. I figure I have to give it a shot, and if it doesn't work, it doesn't work. I'll just accept it."

Roshi responded, "That's the wrong attitude. If they knock you down, you get up. If they knock you down again, get up. No matter how many times they knock you down, get up again. That is how you should go."

The same is true in writing. For every book that makes it, there are probably thousands that don't even get published. We must continue anyway. If you want to write, write. If one book doesn't get published, write another one. Each one will get better because you have all the more practice behind you.

Every other month I am ready to quit writing. The inner dialogue goes something like this: "This is stupid. I am making no money, there's no career in poetry, no one cares about it, it's lonely, I hate it, it's dumb, I want a regular life." These thoughts are torture. Doubt is torture. If we give ourselves fully to something, it will be clearer when it might be appropriate to quit. It is a constant test of perseverance. Sometimes I listen to the doubting voice and get sidetracked for a while. "I think I'll go into sales, open up a café so other writers can go there, sip cappuccino and write, or get married, have babies, be a homemaker and make wonderful chicken dinners."

Don't listen to doubt. It leads no place but to pain and negativity. It is the same with your critic who picks at you while you are trying to write: "That's stupid. Don't say that. Who do you think you are anyway, trying to be a writer?" Don't pay attention to those voices. There is nothing helpful there. Instead, have a tenderness and determination toward your writing, a sense of humor and a deep patience that you are doing the right thing. Avoid getting caught by that small gnawing mouse of doubt. See beyond it to the vastness of life and the belief in time and practice.

A Little Sweet

IN JUDAISM THERE is an old tradition that when a young boy first begins to study, the very first time, after he reads his first word in the Torah, he is given a taste of honey or a sweet. This is so he will always associate learning with sweetness. It should be the same with writing. Right from the beginning, know it is good and pleasant. Don't battle with it. Make it your friend.

And it *is* your friend. It will never desert you, though you may desert it many times. The writing process is a constant source of life and vitality. Sometimes when I come home from work and feel disjointed and blue, I say to myself, "Natalie, you know what you need to do. You need to write." If I'm smart, I listen. If I'm in a destructive or very lazy space, I don't, and the blues continue. But when I do listen, it offers me a chance to touch my life which always softens me and allows me to feel connected with myself again. Even if what I write about is the details of rush hour that morning on the freeway, living them again usually gives me a sense of peace and affirmation: "I'm a human being; I wake up in the morning; I drive on the freeway."

Gore Vidal has a wonderful quote: "As every author—and every reader—knows, writing well is the best trip of them all." Don't even worry about writing "well"; just writing is heaven.

A New Moment

KATAGIRI ROSHI OFTEN used to say: "Take one step off a hundred-foot pole." That's pretty scary, isn't it? Finally you arrive at the top, which is precarious enough, and now you can't stay there. You have to go ahead and step off the edge. In other words, you can't rest on your success. Or your failure. "I have written something wonderful." Good, but it is a new moment. Write something else. Do not be tossed away by your achievements or your fiascoes. Continue under all circumstances. It will keep you healthy and alive. Actually, you don't know for sure that you will fall when you step off the hundred-foot pole. You may fly instead. There are no guarantees one way or the other. Just keep writing.

Tulips come up in spring for no reason. Of course, you planted bulbs and now in April the earth warms up. But why? Because the earth spins around the sun. But why? For no reason except gravity. Why gravity? For no reason. And why did you plant red tulip bulbs to begin with? For beauty, which is itself and has no reason. So the world is empty. Things rise and fall for no reason. And what a great opportunity that is! You can start writing again at any minute. Let go of all your failures and sit down and write something great. Or write something terrible and feel great about it.

Tony Robbins, who teaches workshops in walking on 1,200-degree coals, told a story about a contract that was supposed to be signed. In the past, every time the workshop was scheduled in this particular city, the contractor haggled about the price, schedule, etc. This time Tony decided to change the energy of the interaction. He bought a water pistol, filled it with water, and put it in the inside coat pocket of his thousand-dollar suit. When the argument about money came up, he pulled out the pistol and began shooting it at the contractor across the large office desk on the tenth floor of an executive suite. The contractor was so surprised he began to laugh, saw in a flash that they had been through the same haggle every year, took out his pen, and signed on the black line. Every moment is fresh. Just because a water pistol hasn't been used before at business meetings doesn't mean there is a rule that it can't be used.

Step through your resistances right now and write something great. Right now. This is a new moment.

Why Do I Write?

W HY DO I write?" It's a good question. Ask it of yourself every once in a while. No answer will make you stop writing, and over time you will find that you have given every response.

1. Because I'm a jerk.
2. Because I want the boys to be impressed.
3. So my mother will like me.
4. So my father will hate me.
5. No one listens to me when I speak.
6. So I can start a revolution.
7. In order to write the great American novel and make a million dollars.
8. Because I'm neurotic.
9. Because I'm the reincarnation of William Shakespeare.
10. Because I have something to say.
11. Because I have nothing to say.

Baker Roshi from San Francisco Zen Center said, "'Why?' isn't a good question." Things just are. Hemingway has said, "Not the why, but the what." Give the real detailed information. Leave the why for psychologists. It's enough to know you want to write. Write.

Yet it's a good and haunting question to explore, not so you can find the one final reason, but to see how writing permeates your life with many reasons. Writing is not therapy, though it may have a therapeutic effect. You don't discover that you write because of lack of love and then quit, as you might in therapy discover that you eat chocolate as a love substitute and, seeing the reason, stop (if you're lucky) eating Hershey's chocolate bars and hot fudge. Writing is deeper than therapy. You write *through* your pain, and even your suffering must be written out and let go of.

In writing class painful things come up—the death of a husband, throwing the ashes of a dead baby into a river, a woman going blind. The students read the pieces they just wrote and I tell them they can cry if they need to but to remember to continue to read. We pause when they are finished and then go on to the next person, not because we ignore their suffering—we acknowledge it—but because writing is the aim. It is an opportunity to take the emotions we have felt many times and give them light, color, and a story. We can transform anger into steaming red tulips and sorrow into an old alley full of squirrels in the half light of November.

Writing has tremendous energy. If you find a reason for it, any reason, it seems that rather than negate the act of writing, it makes you burn deeper and glow clearer on the page. Ask yourself, "Why do I write?" or "Why do I want to write?," but don't think about it. Take pen and paper and answer it with clear, assertive statements. Every statement doesn't have to be 100 percent true and each line can contradict the others. Even lie if you need to, to get going. If you don't know why you write, answer it as though you do know why.

Why do I write? I write because I kept my mouth shut all my life and the secret ego truth is I want to live eternally and I want my people to live forever. I hurt at our impermanence, at the passing of time. At the edge of all my joy is the creeping agony that this will pass—this Croissant Express at the corner of Hennepin Avenue in Minneapolis, a great midwestern city in mythical America, will someday stop serving me hot chocolate. I will move on to New Mexico where no one knows how it feels to be here with the sudden light of afternoon, the silver of the ceiling, the half-smell of croissants baking in the oven.

I write because I am alone and move through the world alone. No one will know what has passed through me, and even more amazing, I don't know. Now that it's spring I can't remember what it felt like to be in forty below. Even with the heat on, you could feel mortality screaming through the thin walls of your house.

I write because I am crazy, schizophrenic, and I know it and accept it and I have to do something with it other than go to the loony bin.

I write because there are stories that people have forgotten to tell, because I am a woman trying to stand up in my life. I write because to form a word with your lips and tongue or think a thing and then dare to write it down so you can never take it back is the most powerful thing I know. I am trying to come alive, to find the distances in my own recesses and bring them forward and give them color and form.

I write out of total incomprehension that even love isn't enough and that finally writing might be all I have and that isn't enough. I can never get it all down, and besides, there are times when I have to step away from the table, notebook, and turn to face my own life. Then there are times when it's only coming to the notebook that I truly do face my own life.

And I write out of hurt and how to make hurt okay; how to make myself strong and come home, and it may be the only real home I'll ever have.

This was written at the Croissant Express, April 1984. If I wrote it now, a different response might come up. We write in the moment and reflect our minds, emotions, environment in that moment. This does not mean that one is truer than the other—they are all true.

When the old nag in you comes around with "Why are you wasting your time? Why do you write?," just dive onto the page, be full of answers, but don't try to justify yourself. You do it because you do it. You do it because you want to improve your handwriting, because you're an idiot, because you're mad for the smell of paper.

Every Monday

EVERY MONDAY LAST winter my dear friend Kate and I wrote together. We met at nine in the morning and wrote until about two or three in the afternoon. Sometimes she showed up with an idea: "Let's write about divisions. Okay? Go for an hour." Because there were only the two of us, when the writing sessions were over, we read aloud to each other the whole of what we wrote. It was a lot, with hands moving the whole time.

We tried out writing in different cafés, once even driving an hour south to Owatonna, Minnesota, so I could show her the bank designed by Louis Sullivan that I was in love with. We wrote in the coffee shop across the street. I was unemployed then, looking for a job. She was on a writing grant.

I tell you this because it is important. We were willing to commit ourselves to a whole day of writing each week because writing, sharing, and friendship are important. And it happened on a Monday, the beginning of the work week. Remember this. Remember Kate and me on Mondays when nothing in your life seems worthwhile but earning a living and you find yourself worried about it.

When I was in Jerusalem for three months I had

an Israeli landlady in her fifties. Her TV was broken and she called the repairman. It took him four visits to fix the screen. "But you knew even before he came the first time what was wrong. He could have brought the correct tube and fixed it immediately." She looked at me in astonishment. "Yes, but then we couldn't have had a relationship, sat and drunk tea and discussed the progress of the repairs." Of course, the goal is not to fix a machine but to have relationships.

That is good to remember. What is important is not just what you do—"I am writing a book"—but how you do it, how you approach it, and what you come to value.

A friend living upstairs from me once said, "Natalie, you have relationships with everything, not just with people. You have a relationship with the stairs, your porch, the car, the cornfields, and the clouds." We are a part of everything. When we understand this, we see that we are not writing, but everything is writing through us. Kate and I wrote through each other and through Mondays and through the streets and the coffee. Like bleeding one color into another.

There are many realities. We should remember this when we get too caught in being concerned about the way the rest of the world lives or how we think they live. There is just our lives and how we want to write and how we want to touch the rain, the table, the music, paper cups and pine trees.

A good warm-up or awakener is to write for ten

minutes, beginning with "I am a friend to . . ." and only list inanimate objects. It helps to bring those things into the scope of our lives. The toaster, the highway, the mountains, the curb, live with us too. Doing this exercise and writing with a friend remind us to step outside ourselves when we are stuck too deep into ourselves.

More About Mondays

I WANT TO talk more about those Mondays with Kate. One time we met at her house on the first floor, her husband asleep upstairs and the children at day care, a space heater on the massage table—not helping my cold hands much. We smoked cigarette after cigarette, not inhaling but "playing smoking." Kate had a scarf wrapped around her neck like they do in New York.

We talked about our voices as writers—how they are strong and brave but how as people we are wimps. This is what creates our craziness. The chasm between the great love we feel for the world when we sit and write about it and the disregard we give it in our own human lives. How Hemingway could write of the great patience of Santiago in the fishing boat and how Hemingway himself, when he stepped out of his writing studio, mistreated his wife and drank too much. We have to begin to bring these two worlds together. Art is the act of nonaggression. We have to live this art in our daily lives.

We spent the whole day mostly talking, only getting around to two twenty-minute writing sessions and a beautiful poem by Kenneth Rexroth, but that was okay. The whole day was a good poem. Friendship, cold feet, feeding the cat, filling the ashtray with cigarette butts. And if we were smart it would have continued into Monday night when we left each other and were alone in our separate worlds.

Katagiri Roshi says, "Our goal is to have kind consideration for all sentient beings every moment forever." This does not mean put a good poem on paper and then spit at our lives, curse our cars, and cut off someone on the freeway. It means carry the poem away from the desk and into the kitchen. That is how we will survive as writers, no matter how little money we make in the American economy and how little acceptance we get in the magazines. We are not writing for money and acceptance—although that would be nice.

The deepest secret in our heart of hearts is that we are writing because we love the world, and why not finally carry that secret out with our bodies into the living rooms and porches, backyards and grocery stores? Let the whole thing flower: the poem and the person writing the poem. And let us always be kind in this world.

Spontaneous Writing Booths

D O NOT FEEL left out when your school, church, Zen center, daycare center has a bazaar, carnival, rummage sale. Don't think you have nothing to contribute. Simply set up a spontaneous writing booth. All you need is a pile of blank paper, some fast-writing pens, a table, a chair, and a sign saying, "Poems on Demand" or "Poems in the Moment" or "You name the subject, I'll write on it."

I did this for three years for the Summer Festival and Bazaar at the Minnesota Zen Center. I timidly began charging fifty cents a poem, but by the next year it was up to a dollar. There was a waiting line throughout the day. I let my customers give me any topic. Some were "the sky," "emptiness," "Minnesota," and of course "love." Kids wanted poems on purple, their shoes, bellies. My rule was that I filled one side of a piece of standard-size paper, did not cross out, nor did I stop to reread it. I also didn't worry about putting what I said in poetic stanzas. I filled a page like I did in my notebook. It was another form of writing practice.

In Japan there are stories of great Zen poets writing a superb haiku and then putting it in a bottle in a river or nearby stream and letting it go. For anyone who is a writer, this is a profound example of nonattachment. The spontaneous poetry booth is the twentieth-century equivalent. It is practice in unselfconsciousness. Write, don't reread it, let it go into the world. There were several times when I felt I really hit home in the writing, but I just handed the sheet of paper over to the customer across the table and went on.

Chögyam Trungpa has said that you have to be a great warrior to be a business person. You must be fearless and willing to lose everything at any moment. With the writing booth there is the opportunity to be a great warrior: you must let go of everything as you write and then in handing it over to the customer. When you work that fast there is a real loss of control. I always said much more than I wanted to say. I feared a child would ask me to write a sweet piece about jelly beans and I'd zip over to how your gut turns green, red, or blue depending on the particular bean you are eating.

But we should never underestimate people. They do desire the cut of truth. The booth was extremely popular. Though American society does not particularly support poets and writers, there is a secret dream and respect for the act of writing. Ten years ago when I lived in Taos, New Mexico, I rented a run-down adobe for fifty dollars a month. The landlord had been born in the house thirty-six years ago, hated it, and was now an up-and-coming middle-class insurance agent living in Albuquerque. He scorned anyone who chose to live in that environment. I loved the house with the zeal of a foreigner. I didn't care that it had an outhouse, one cold-water spigot, and wood-burning stoves. I tried many times to be friendly to my landlord when he came from the big city in his big car, but nothing seemed to work. We were in two different worlds.

One day I received a very thick envelope from him sent special delivery. I thought, "Uh-oh! He's going to raise the rent." (Every time I made an improvement, he raised the rent.) When I opened the packet, the first thing I saw was an article torn from a local newspaper about a poetry reading I had given the previous week. As soon as I saw that, I thought, "Uh-oh! I'm being evicted." Instead, I read a letter from Tony Garcia saying, "Dear Natalie, I see that you are a poet. Enclosed are twenty-five poems I have written over the last ten years. Please read them at your next poetry reading." In my wildest dreams I never thought of using poetry as a way to connect with him!

One year ago I received a letter from a man in San Francisco who wrote that he had been pretty mixed up and joined the Coast Guard. He only brought two things on board with him: photos of his family and the poem I had written him three years ago at the bazaar in Minnesota. Now he said he was doing well, making money with computers. He asked me if I was short on cash and said if I was, he would love to send me some money. He wrote that he always kept the poem folded in his wallet.

Frankly, I have no idea what I wrote in that poem, but I hope it said something good about the huge maple trees above our heads that afternoon, the light on the lake across the street, the sound of roller skates, the distant playing of a sax, and how good it was to be there that summer in Minnesota.

Having a writing booth is excellent practice in letting go. Let go completely. Let yourself totally be a writer from now on.

A Sensation of Space

W HEN YOU WANT to write in a certain form—a
novel, short story, poem—read a lot of writing
in that form. Watch how that form is paced. What is
the first sentence? What makes it finished? When you
read a lot in that form, it becomes imprinted inside
you, so when you sit down to write, you write in that
structure. For instance, if you are a poet and want to
write a novel, you have to learn to write full sentences
and not leap from one image to another. In reading
novels your body digests full sentences, the steady
hand of setting scenes, knowing the color of the tablecloth and how the writer gets her character to move
across the room to the coffeepot.

If you want to write short poems, you must digest
that form and then exercise in that form. Try this:
write a series of ten short poems. You only have three
minutes to write each one; each one must be three
lines. Begin each one with a title that you choose
from something your eye falls on: for example, glass,
salt, water, light reflecting, the window. Three lines,
three minutes, the first title is "Glass." Without thinking, write three deft lines. Pause a moment. Do another. Three minutes, three lines, the title is "Salt."

Continue in this way until that short thinking is a structure inside you and you can call it forth when that's the form you need. Especially in a short poem, all words are used economically and the title should add another dimension to the poem rather than repeat a word already used in the body of the short poem.

Tony Robbins, the fire-walker, says that when you want to learn something, go to experts who have put in thirty years and learn from them. Study their belief systems, their mental syntax—the order in which they think—and their physiology, how they stand, breathe, hold their mouth when they do the task they are expert in. In other words, model them. So when you go to break wood, you are not you, you are the black belt in karate that you have been modeling, and your hand does not stop at wood but goes through it.

So this is good but it is very tricky. Form alone will not create art. For instance, we are taught that a haiku is a Japanese short poem form. It has seventeen syllables and is written in three lines. It often mentions a season and something from nature. Children in elementary schools all over the United States are taught to write these three-line poems, but in truth, they are not haiku. If you sit down and read a lot of Basho, Shiki, Issa, Buson, four of the greatest Haiku masters, in good translation by R. H. Blyth, you will see that, in fact, his translations do not even follow the form of seventeen syllables with five syllables in the first line, seven in the second, and five in the third. Japanese is a very different language from English. Each syllable in Japanese carries a lot more weight than it does in English, so in order to write haiku in English, just use three short lines. "Okay. I've got it. I've studied Blyth's translations. It's three short lines to make haiku, and I can skip the syllable count." Yes, but then what makes it haiku and not just a short poem?

If you read a lot of haiku, you see there is a leap that happens, a moment where the poet makes a large jump and the reader's mind must catch up. This creates a little sensation of space in the reader's mind, which is nothing less than a moment's experience of God, and when you feel it, there is usually an "Aah" wanting to issue from your lips. Try reading these, translated by R. H. Blyth.[15] Take your time and pause after each one.

> Among the grasses,
> A flower blooms white,
> Its name unknown.
>
> — SHIKI

> Spring departs,
> Trembling, in the grasses
> Of the fields.
>
> — ISSA

The scent and colour
Of the wisteria
Seem far from the moon.

— BUSON

The voice of the pheasant;
How I longed
For my dead parents!

— BASHO

That sensation of space is a true test of haiku. No matter how well we learn to write three-line poems, it takes much practice to fill those three lines with an experience of God. Basho has said that if you write five haiku in your life, you are a haiku writer, and if you write ten, you are a master.

We may write three novels before we write a good one. So form is important, we should learn form, but we should also remember to fill form with life. This takes practice.

A Large Field to Wander In

THREE SUMMERS AGO David took an intensive week-long workshop with me in northern Minnesota. There were twenty students in the workshop. Several of the students were teachers who had the time off; others were adults who had regular careers in other fields. They all had an interest in writing, though many were timid and very nervous the first morning of class. I gave them the usual pep talk about trusting their own voices and saying what they needed to say. Then we wrote for ten minutes, and went around the circle and read what we had written. People were shaking as they read, not necessarily because they had written anything earth-shattering this first morning, but because it is very naked to put your voice out there for the first time in a group of strangers. People read about their childhoods, their farm, how nervous they were. It was a regular beginning. Then David read in a very loud voice:

Masturbation. Masturbation. Maaaaaaas... Ma! Ma! Ma! Ma! Mastur ba ba ba tion tion tion...

And so forth. It certainly woke everyone up. David wrote little else on any other subject for the entire week. Now, on the basis of that kind of writing, one would wonder why I had a great belief in his ability, but I did. Right from the beginning he broke all rules of syntax, said what he needed to, and continued to trust his own voice to all our amazement. I also felt great energy from his writing and knew if he could harness it—why, he could even move on to other subjects. As he came to writing groups during the next two years, I was impressed by his determination, and I loved his sense of humor (though at times I was the only one laughing in the group). It is true that often no one could quite understand what he was talking about, but I trusted the energy behind his words.

Often I have had students who were very coherent right from the beginning. They wrote complete sentences, were descriptive, detailed, and grounded. In Minnesota, in the heart of the Midwest, almost everyone could write like this. I heard stories about tornadoes, winters, grandmothers, but after years of that I felt there was nowhere to go in their writing. Because they did write well, they were unwilling to leave what they knew, to break into new frontiers and crack open their world into the unknown. I remember in one Tuesday-night class, the writing was so basically solid and good, I couldn't shake them. I wanted them to foam at the mouth, becoming blithering idiots, and wander into unknown fields. At the end of the class, after they were eager to understand and didn't, and I was eager to shake them and couldn't, I suddenly stopped and said, "I know what the problem is! None of you have ever taken acid!"

Now, I don't propose that LSD or psychedelics necessarily make a person a better writer. What I meant was at some point in our lives we have to be crazy, we have to lose control, step out of our ordinary way of seeing, and learn that the world is not the way we think it is, that it isn't solid, structured, and forever. We are going to die someday, and nothing can control it. Don't take LSD. Go to the woods alone for three days. If you are terrified of horses, buy one and make friends with it. Extend your boundaries. Live on the edge for a while. We act as though we were immortal, and are comfortable in that illusion. We don't actually know when we will die and we hope it will be in old age, but it can be this next minute. This thought of mortality is not droll; it can make our lives very vital, present, and alert right now.

I trusted that while David was out there flying in his writing, he would land someday and make his vision clear to us who were living in the solid land of Minnesota. He would down-spiral and hit the mark exactly like a great archer. He had given himself a lot of space. If you begin too exactly, you will stay precise but never hit the exact mark that makes the words vibrate with the truth that goes through the present, past, and future.

The important thing is that David was determined and he continued. I was only half surprised when he just recently entered a master's program in writing at the University of Minnesota so he could learn to write in full sentences and to write persuasive essays and memoirs, and so his energy could come home to roost. And it did with pieces like this:

Legs

BY DAVID LIEBERMAN

Looking at the photo of Gerald Stern and Jack Gilbert
on the cover of the *Red Coal*—
The way Gerald walks
I love him,
I love his body,
the way his legs fill the baggy pants,
make them stand like lions,
his walk like his mind is open and
spinning on all the juice of Paris,
shimmering legs, like Art Deco,
like slender tanks,
legs with mind.
I love Gerald Stern walking in Paris 1950.
And myself walking in the Mission, San Francisco
February with Don
and the young Mexican men and the women too
challenging the universe with their legs.
Only in cities do you see this
where the body chemically absorbs

all of the power of the streets and
shops and cars and trolleys and noises
and the hundred ways they are organized
and disorganized in sound and vision and smell
and it all comes up like steam
from the subway grates
and is collected in men's bodies
and liberates their minds.

Suzuki Roshi says in *Zen Mind, Beginner's Mind* that "The best way to control people is to encourage them to be mischievous. Then they will be in control in its wider sense. To give your sheep or cow a large, spacious meadow is the way to control him." You need a large field in writing too. Don't pull in the reins too quickly. Give yourself tremendous space to wander in, to be utterly lost with no name, and then come back and speak.

The Goody Two-Shoes Nature

IN ORDER TO improve your writing, you have to practice just like any other sport. But don't be dutiful and make it into a blind routine. "Yes, I have written an hour today and I wrote an hour yesterday and an hour the day before." Don't just put in your time. That is not enough. You have to make great effort. Be willing to put your whole life on the line when you sit down for writing practice. Otherwise you are just mechanically pushing the pen across the page and intermittently looking at the clock to see if your time is up.

Some people hear the rule "Write every day" and do it and don't improve. They are just being dutiful. That is the way of the Goody Two-shoes. It is a waste of energy because it takes tremendous effort to just follow the rules if your heart isn't into it. If you find that this is your basic attitude, then stop writing. Stay away from it for a week or a year. Wait until you are hungry to say something, until there is an aching in you to speak. Then come back.

Don't worry. You won't have lost time. Your energy will be more direct and less wasted. This does not mean "Great, I'll stay away for a little while and then come back wanting to do it and I won't have any more trouble." There will always be trouble, but the embers of expression deep inside you will have had some space and air to really begin to glow. You will have made a deeper commitment and come back more fully choosing to engage.

It is also good to remember that if you have been pushing hard for a while—a few weeks, a month, a whole weekend nonstop—rest completely for a while. Do something totally different and stop thinking about writing. Go paint the living room that looks dark and ugly; paint it white. Try baking some of the desserts that you cut out the recipes for in your local newspaper. Put full energy into something else. Do your taxes or play with your kids totally for two weeks. You will learn about your own rhythm—when you need to write and when you need to rest. This will give you a deeper relationship with yourself. You won't follow rules blindly.

I am thinking of the very close friend whom I traveled with in Europe for a month. She was very busy teaching during the year and raising her four-year-old son. This month in Europe she was determined to write an hour a day. It was very painful to watch her because she approached it as dutifully as she did her teaching, her evening cooking, her laundry.

As we talked, I found out she had never missed one day of school in her entire public school career. Even if she was sick, her mother insisted she go to school. We have been taught to follow rules and never think about the value of the rules. Over my six years in Minnesota I met several people who proudly told me they had perfect attendance in public school. I fail to see the real value of perfect attendance. Yes, schools receive a daily allowance from the government for student attendance, and there is virtue in dependability, perseverance, and regularity. These qualities should be taught, but not in a black-and-white way.

There should also be shades of gray and blue. There are dentist appointments, sadness over the death of a dog, Jewish holidays or American Indian celebrations, sore throats, a visit from your grandmother. Life is very big. There should be a flexibility in our daily routines so we have the space to feel how good it is to receive a public school education and learn to read words and form letters with our yellow pencils on white, blue-lined paper.

You need this flexibility and space also for writing. Writing asks you to be engaged. Yes, after an hour of keeping your hand moving, you will have several pages filled with words; but ultimately, you can't fool yourself. You must enter the gray and blue and your feelings, hopes, dreams. Somewhere along you have to break through. If not in this writing session, then in the next. If you are bored for years of writing, it means you are not connecting with yourself and the process. If you have a wish hidden below your Goody Two-shoes nature to be a writer but you make effort only as far as putting in your time, it just isn't enough.

Sometimes you have to change something else in your life in order to go further. Writing alone is not enough. One night in the Milan airport, after we had each had a glass of wine, my friend asked me, "Well, do you think I'll be a writer?" I had to say the truth. "Well, I think you will have a good life, bring up a good kid, and have a happy marriage. I don't know if you'll be a writer." She slammed down her glass and said with more energy and original response than she had the whole trip thus far, "I'm not going to finish out my life cooking hot dogs on Sundays!" When the month was over she had firmly decided to quit her eleven-year-old teaching job, which she had been tired of for the last few years, and try something absurd that she had always wanted to do—be a bartender. Her writing the last days of the trip was full of vitality.

When I lived in the Midwest I loved to walk in cornfields. I would drive out to farmland, park my car, and walk in the rows of cornfields for hours. In fall you could hear the dry stalks crack. When I invited a friend to join me, her immediate response was, "But isn't that illegal? Doesn't someone own that field?" Yes, very strictly speaking that is true, but I didn't hurt anything. No one ever seemed to mind, and on several occasions when I met the farmers who owned the fields, they were accepting of what I did and mildly amused that I took joy in their fields.

It is important to feel out the situation. Do not

make up your own rules ahead of time. If there had been barbed wire around the fields, I would have read the clear message. Rather than following rules, have a friendliness toward existence. Rules were made so things won't be hurt or abused. If you are kind, you will naturally be doing the right thing without having to refer to legalities. I knew not to pick the corn or step on the roots, and I walked between the rows.

Don't be a Goody Two-shoes just to be a Goody Two-shoes. It is not based on any reality. Go into the cornfields. Go into your writing with your whole heart. Don't set up a system—"I have to write every day"—and then numbly do it.

But please note: just as with my friend who had to change her life in order to go deeper into her writing, the reverse is also true. You can't go deep into your writing and then step out of it, clamp down, go home, "be nice," and not speak the truth. If you give yourself over to honesty in your practice, it will permeate your life.

You can't straighten up during writing and then hunch back down when you let go of the pen. Writing can teach us the dignity of speaking the truth, and it spreads out from the page into all of our life, and it should. Otherwise, there is too much of a schism between who we are as writers and how we live our daily lives. That is the challenge: to let writing teach us about life and life about writing. Let it flow back and forth.

No Hindrances

I WAS AT a wedding in Taos, New Mexico, talking
with a person I knew ten years ago at the Lama
Foundation. I remembered that he had tilled and
planted a whole bean crop by hand that summer.
He is a builder now and says he knows if he did the
dead center of what he's supposed to be doing, it
would be writing, "but building's easier." I told him
about this book and how the day before I'd had the
worst resistance to writing I ever had. "I wanted to
scream and burn my typewriter. I never wanted to
write again."

"Yeah, but what else is there to do?" he asked,
looking me straight in the eye.

"Nothing."—And I knew it was true.

When you accept writing as what you are supposed
to do, after you've tried everything else—marriage,
hippiedom, traveling, living in Minnesota or New
York, teaching, spiritual practices—there's finally no
place else to go. So no matter how big the resistance,
there is one day, there is the next day, and the writing
work ahead. You can't depend on its going smoothly
day after day. It won't be that way. You might have one
day that is superb, productive, and the next time you

write, you are ready to sign up on a ship headed for Saudi Arabia. There are no guarantees. You might think you have finally created a rhythm with three days running, and the next day the needle scratches the record and you squeak through it, teeth on edge.

See the big picture. You are committed to writing or finding out about it. Continue under all circumstances. Don't be rigid, though. If one day you have to take your kids to the dentist when it is your time to write, write in the dentist's office or don't write. Just stay in touch underneath with your commitment for this wild, silly, and wonderful writing practice. Always stay friendly toward it. It's easier to come back to a good friend than an enemy. Dogen, a thirteenth-century Zen Buddhist master, said, "Every day is a good day." That is the ultimate attitude we should have toward our writing, even if we have good *and* bad days.

Two years ago I won a writing fellowship. I had a year and a half off to just write. I never could find a rhythm that worked for longer than four or five days. I tried writing from nine in the morning to one in the afternoon. That worked and then it didn't. I tried two to six. That was good for a while. Then, whenever I wanted to write. That was okay, on and off. Each week I varied my schedule. I had the opportunity to try all times of the day and night. Nothing ever became perfect. The important thing was never to give up the relationship with writing, no matter how many different tactics I may have tried.

Think of writing as though it were breathing. Just because you have to plant a garden or take the subway or teach a class, you don't stop inhaling and exhaling. That's how basic writing is, too. Here's something I found in my notebook, written July 27, 1984:

I know this working with my tired, resistant brain is the deepest I'll get on the earth. Not the joy or ecstasy I feel sometimes or the momentary flashes of enlightenment, but this touching of the nitty-gritty of my everyday life and standing in it and continuing to write is what breaks my heart open so deeply to a tenderness and soft-ness toward myself and from that, a glowing compassion for all that is around me. Not just for the table and Coke in front of me, the paper straw, air conditioner, men crossing the street on this July day in Norfolk, Nebraska, bank digital clock blinking 4:03, my friend writing opposite me, but for the swirling memories and deep longings of our minds and the suffering we work through daily. And it comes from me naturally as I move pen across the page and break down the hard, solid crusts of thought in my own mind and the way I limit myself.

So it is very deep to be a writer. It is the deepest thing I know. And I think, if not this, nothing— it will be my way in the world for the rest of my life. I have to remember this again and again.

A Meal You Love

I F YOU FIND you are having trouble writing and nothing seems real, just write about food. It is always solid and is the one thing we all can remember about our day. I had a writing group once that just couldn't get off the ground. Every exercise ended in bland writing. Then one day I had an idea: "Okay, you have ten minutes. Write about a meal you love." The writing was vibrant, full of colorful details. No abstractions. There was energy in the room. When it comes to food, people know what they like, are definite, concrete, explicit.

Diane DiPrima, a Beat Generation poet, wrote a book entitled *Dinners and Nightmares*. The whole first half of the book tells of meals she's eaten, suppers she's made, guest lists for the suppers, shopping lists for the meals. There's a wonderful story about the time she spent a whole winter in New York City eating Oreo cookies. It's good reading. You never get bored. We all love to eat.

Write about the foods you love most. Be specific. Give us the details. Where did you eat it, who were you with, what season was it in? What was the best meal you had last week? "That banana I ate in the cold kitchen Tuesday morning stopped the world."

From the table, the cheese, the old blue-eyed friend across from you, from the glasses of water, the striped tablecloth, fork, knife, thick white plate, green salad, butter, and glass of pale pink wine, you can extend yourself out in memory, time, space, thought, to Israel, Russia, to religion, the trees and the sidewalk. And you have a place to begin from, something concrete, palatable, clear, right in front of your face.

Okay, so some of you may not be social. You've never eaten a good meal in your life, you're broke and don't have any friends. Well, simply begin with the last stale cheese sandwich you had in that empty apartment on First Avenue with the cockroaches floating on the top of your two-day-old coffee. It's your life, begin from it.

Use Loneliness

L AST NIGHT I was sitting with a very old friend in my living room. "You know, Natalie, I know you've talked about being lonely, but last week when I was really lonely, I felt that I was the only person in the world who ever felt it." That's what loneliness is about. If we felt connected to people, even other lonely people, we wouldn't feel alone anymore.

When I was separated from my husband, Katagiri Roshi said to me, "You should live alone. You should learn about that. It is the terminal abode."

"Roshi, will I get used to loneliness?"

"No, you don't get used to it. I take a cold shower every morning and every morning it shocks me, but I continue to stand up in the shower. Loneliness always has a bite, but learn to stand up in it and not be tossed away."

Later that year I went to Roshi again: "It's really hard. I come home and I'm alone and I get panicky." He asked me what I did when I was alone. Suddenly, it had a fascination. "Well, I wash the dishes, I daydream and doodle on pieces of paper, draw hearts and color them in. I pick the dead leaves off the plants and I listen to music a lot." I began to study my own desolation and I became interested in it. I stopped fighting it.

Writing can be very lonely. Who's going to read it, who cares about it? A student asked me, "Do you write for yourself or do you write for an audience?" Think of sharing your need to talk with someone else when you write. Reach out of the deep chasm of loneliness and express yourself to another human being. "This is how it was for me when I lived in the Midwest." Write so they understand. Art is communication. Taste the bitterness of isolation, and from that place feel a kinship and compassion for all people who have been alone. Then in your writing lead yourself out of it by thinking of someone and wanting to express your life to him. Reach out in your writing to another lonely soul. "This is how I felt when I drove across Nebraska, late August, early evening alone in my blue car."

Use loneliness. Its ache creates urgency to reconnect with the world. Take that aching and use it to propel you deeper into your need for expression—to speak, to say who you are and how you care about light and rooms and lullabies.

Blue Lipstick and a Cigarette Hanging Out Your Mouth

SOMETIMES THERE IS just no way around it—we are boring and we are sick of ourselves, our voice, and the usual material we write about. It's obvious that if even going to a café to write doesn't help, it is time to find other ways. Dye your hair green, paint your nails purple, get your nose pierced, dress as the opposite sex, perm your hair.

Actually, one small prop can often tip your mind into another place. When I sit down to write, often I have a cigarette hanging out of my mouth. If I'm in a café that has a "No Smoking" sign, then my cigarette is unlit. I don't actually smoke anyway, so it doesn't matter. The cigarette is a prop to help me dream into another world. It wouldn't work so well if I ordinarily smoked. You need to do something you don't usually do.

Borrow your friend's black leather motorcycle jacket, walk across the coffee shop like a Hell's Angel, and sit down and write. Put on a beret or house shoes and a nightgown, wear work boots, farmer's overalls, a three-piece suit, wrap yourself in an American flag or wear curlers in your hair. Just sit down to write in a state you don't ordinarily sit down to write in. Try writing on a large drawing pad. Wear all white and a stethoscope around your neck—whatever it takes to simply see the world from another angle.

Going Home

I WANTED TO say when I saw her art show in New York that something was missing. She needed to go back to North Platte, Nebraska, where she came from. She needed to complete the circle." I overheard this. One friend was telling another.

It is very important to go home if you want your work to be whole. You don't have to move in with your parents again and collect a weekly allowance, but you must claim where you come from and look deep into it. Come to honor and embrace it, or at the least, accept it.

I had a writing friend who was married to a man of Italian descent. She always wrote about his family and their conversations at the dinner table. I told her, "It's great stuff, but I don't quite trust it until I hear about your family, too. Tell me what it's like to be white, Protestant, upper-middle-class. I honestly don't know." Often we can look to someone else's life as interesting and our life as dull. We lose our center and are lopsided because we are looking for something we think we don't have. We act like hungry ghosts. This does not mean that we should only write about ourselves, but we should be able to look outside ourselves with a sense of generosity. "I am rich and they are rich."

I was a Zen student for many years, and then about a year and a half ago every time I sat zazen I felt more and more Jewish. When I spoke to Katagiri Roshi about this, he said, "That makes sense. The more you sit, the more you become who you are." I began to feel that I had been arrogant to turn my back on my own heritage without knowing anything about it.

Where you come from affects your writing. Even in the patterns of language. I often unconsciously have written in the rhythm of Hebrew prayers and chants, using that repetition. Though my family wasn't religious, at the High Holy Days I was present when people were davening (praying and swaying their bodies). A young child is very impressionable. That is when the rhythm of language enters her body. I have heard it said that it is not what poets say but their ability to tune in to certain language rhythms that makes them great.

When you do practice writing there are often times when you hook into a form, a certain way you heard a church service every Sunday or the beats of rock 'n' roll or an auctioneer at the state fair where you were a 4-H-er. You don't write the words of the church litany, but you fill that pattern that is imprinted in you with your own words and feelings. That pattern can give you a vehicle for expression. It is like plugging into an electric circuit.

Also, there are charming ways your family and region speak. Get to know that; appreciate it. "Well, blue corn!" a man in Texas said to me when he saw how heavy my backpack was. When I asked a ridiculous question, my grandmother said, "Does a horse lay oranges?" Make a list of all the expressions your family uses and incorporate them in your writing.

But don't go home so you can stay there. You go home so you can be free; so you are not avoiding anything of who you are. If you avoid something, it becomes obvious in your writing. For example, if you are uncomfortable with sexuality, it becomes clear because either your writing never mentions it, as though all your characters, animals, and insects had sexual lobotomies, or you go to the other extreme and always write about whores and porno flicks. You want to find a middle road, a place where you are comfortable.

We hear about people who go back to their roots. That is good, but don't get stuck in the root. There is the branch, the leaf, the flower—all reaching toward the immense sky. We are many things. In Israel looking for my "roots," I realized that while I was a Jew, I was also an American, a feminist, a writer, a Buddhist. We are products of the modern era—it is our richness and our dilemma. We are not one thing. Our roots are becoming harder to dig out. Yet they are important and the ones most easy to avoid because there is often pain embedded there—that's why we left in the first place.

When I first moved to Minnesota, Jim White, a very fine poet, said to me, "Whatever you do, don't become a regional writer." Don't get caught in the trap of becoming provincial. While you write about the cows of Iowa, how they stand and bend to chew, feel compassion simultaneously for the cows in Russia, in Czechoslovakia, for their eventual death and for their flanks cooked and served in stews, in bowls and on plates, to feed people on both sides of the earth. Go into your region, but don't stop there. Let it pique your curiosity to examine and look closely at more of the world.

When I began to study Judaism, I couldn't just stay with the religious prayers. I felt compelled to face the pain of the Holocaust, the history of Israel, and the whole story of the wandering of my people. Through that I was able for the first time to feel great empathy for political movements and the struggle of human beings outside America. In the ability to connect with one people lies the chance to feel compassion for all people. In Israel I felt how hard life was, not only for the Jews, but I understood too that the Arabs suffered. Looking into my roots made me come to feel anguish for anyone who walked that soil.

So go home. Not so you can boast, "My uncle was a colonel in World War II," but so you can penetrate quietly and clearly into your own people and from that begin to understand all people and their struggles.

All writers, at some level, want to be known. That's

why they speak. Here is a chance to bring your reader deeper into your heart. You can explain with deep knowledge what it means to be a Catholic, a man, a southerner, a black person, a woman, a homosexual, a human being. You know it better than anyone else. In knowing who you are and writing from it, you will help the world by giving it understanding.

A Story Circle

There were several times in Taos that I called a story-telling circle. I invited friends from the surrounding hills of Talpa, Carson, Arroyo Hondo, and Arroyo Seco to gather in my home. We sat in a circle on the floor. Next door you could hear the bells on Shel's goats, and I knew that Bill Montoyo was once again sneaking his sheep near our garden where they could graze on the unusually long pigweed that grew there.

I lit a candle in the middle of our circle of about ten people. Lighting a candle helps to create a sense of magic. Then I asked them, "Okay, tell me about a time you were really happy." At other circles I've asked, "Tell us about a place you really love" or "a time you were really down," or "Tell us the most extraordinary story you know" or "a story you love to tell," or "Give us a magic moment that you remember from last week."

We went around the circle. Stories stay with us. It is seven years later and I still remember them.

Rick: There was a big elm in the backyard of my childhood home in Larchmont, New York. I was six and would climb to almost the top, to my favorite branch. It was late fall with no leaves on the trees. I lay down on my favorite branch and wrapped my arms around it. I closed my eyes and the wind blew and my branch, which was big, swayed and I swayed with it. I will always remember that feeling of being in love with that tree.

LAUCHLAN: There was one summer that I was a forest ranger in Oregon for four months. I was alone for that whole time and I hardly ever wore any clothes that summer, because there was no one around. I was deep in the woods. By the end of the summer I was very tan and very calm. It was late August and I was squatting, picking the berries off a berry bush and eating them. Suddenly I felt a tongue licking my shoulder and I slowly turned my head. There was a deer licking the sweat on my back! I didn't move. Then she moved next to me and together we silently ate berries off the bush. I was stunned. An animal trusted me that much!

JOSEPH: This story isn't directly about me. It's about a friend of mine's roommate. I'll call him Bill. Bill was from France. He was a bit weird, definitely out of balance. He was working with dolphins in New York, really loved them. We called him the Scientist. It was the early days of LSD. We called it lysergic acid back then. Some of us were experimenting with it. We were careful not to do it around the Scientist, because we were afraid he would take it and really go off the edge.

Well, one time he took some, I don't know how he got his hands on it, but anyway, he did take some. We all thought, "Uh-oh!" but we tried to relax. He put on his jacket—it was night—and left the apartment. He walked down to where he worked, went in, and stood watching the dolphins in the pool. He swears that the female started to look like Marilyn Monroe and grew breasts, had on lipstick, and beckoned him to join her in the pool. He said he took off all his clothes and dove in and made love with her. He swore he did. We were all very weirded out when we heard about it, and my friend who was his roommate soon moved out.

I think this could be really true because several years later I was living with friends on Venice Beach, California. We were taking acid all the time then. It was the middle sixties and we decorated our whole house in bright psychedelic colors. The bathroom was avocado green, and we had a fishbowl in there with two goldfish. One day I dropped some acid and was walking on the beach. I came back to the house and went into the bathroom and looked at the goldfish. One of them suddenly became Brigitte Bardot. Spontaneously, I stuck my hand in the bowl, grabbed the fish by the tail, and swallowed her whole before I even know what I was doing! I was amazed.

BRETT: I visited my grandmother Chloe in Kankakee, Illinois. She was eighty-two at the time and I hadn't seen her in four years. I was crazy about her and was really excited to see her. The visit was going to be a surprise. I hitched down from Minnesota, where I was living then. When I got to her house, which was across the street from Dunkin' Donuts, she was in the backyard leaning over some red snapdragons. I yelled, "Chloe!" She turned around and said, "Oh, Brett, come here a minute. I want to show you something." I went over and she pressed a snapdragon together to show me how it could look like a bunny rabbit. Then she took my hand and led me over to her two peach trees. "I'm gonna make peach preserves outta these." "Chloe, you haven't seen me in four years." She reached up and picked a peach off the tree and held it up so I could inspect it: "I know, honey. I've missed you." Then we went in the house and she fed me some of her famous dumplings and talked to me about the neighbors and my father and how she wished he would go to church. She talked to me like I had never been gone.

These four stories I remember vividly. Our stories are important. Try calling a story circle with some friends. All you need is a candle. You don't need drugs or alcohol. Once the stories begin, they are all the enchantment you would want. Then later, on your own, write your stories down. To begin with, write like you talk, nothing fancy. This will help you get started.

Writing Marathons

USUALLY AT THE end of an eight-week writing workshop which meets once a week for two hours, we have a four-hour writing marathon. You don't necessarily need a class to do a marathon. I have done it for a whole day with just one other person. This is how it works: Everyone in the group agrees to commit himself or herself for the full time. Then we make up a schedule. For example, a ten-minute writing session, another ten-minute session, a fifteen-minute session, two twenty-minute sessions, and then we finish with a half-hour round of writing. So for the first session we all write for ten minutes and then go around the room and read what we have written with no comments by anyone. If the class is too large and it will take up too much time, we alternate the people who will read after each round, so you might read every other time instead of every time. A pause naturally happens after each reader, but we do not say "That was great" or even "I know what you mean." There is no good or bad, no praise or criticism. We read what we have written and go on to the next person. People are allowed to pass and not read twice during the marathon. Naturally there should be flexibility. If someone feels the need to pass more often or less often, that is fine. What usually happens is you stop thinking: you write; you read; you write; you become less and less self-conscious. Everyone is in the same boat, and because no comments are made, you feel freer and freer to write anything you want.

After a while your voice begins to feel disembodied; you are not sure if you said something or someone across the room said it. Because there are no comments, if someone writes something you want to respond to, you can address that person in the next writing round: "Bev, I know what you mean. My parents argued too under the kitchen lights with the dinner half eaten and the green linoleum spread out across the floor." Not commenting on another person's work builds up a healthy desire to speak. You can pour that energy into your next round of writing. Write, read, write, read. It is an excellent way to cut through the internal censor and to give yourself tremendous space to write whatever's on your mind.

We also have a box in the center of the room where people put in topic suggestions folded on pieces of paper. At the beginning of each round of writing, someone pulls out a slip of paper and reads the topic. You don't necessarily have to write on it, but if you are stuck you can begin from there. You'll be surprised that once you are in that automatic state, you can write on any topic. Or you might use the topic as a jumping-off place to get your hand moving: "'Swimming.' I am a great swimmer and very confident. There. Now what I really want to write about is how I will turn into white light someday. . . ." Or you can think there is nothing to say about swimming, begin to write, and remember how you adored Esther Williams when you were very young, sitting next to your father in the movie theater, hand dripping with the butter from your popcorn.

People are nervous the first time they do a marathon. They fear they won't have anything to say or can't keep writing for that long. They are amazed when it is done that the time went so quickly—"I could have written all day!" Once, at a week-long workshop for the University of Minnesota, I had twelve students try a marathon the first morning. In the beginning they were resistant and sneered at me. When it was finished, one man chimed in, "Let's have lunch and then do another marathon in the afternoon." For the entire week we did nothing else. We tried beginning some rounds at ten at night and writing until one in the morning or starting at seven in the morning and writing until noon.

During that week someone pulled "Your first sexual experience" out of the topic box. That topic set up one woman for the rest of the week. She wrote about her first sexual experience, her second, her third, and so on. I believe she is still in Hill City, Minnesota, at the Rainbow Tavern writing about her

708th sexual experience. The high school students are playing pool nearby, and she continues to order Pepsi so she can hold her booth in the tavern. She doesn't know whether it is night or day, and her hand keeps moving across the page. Surely she will become enlightened any time now, and we wonder, "Will she ever return, will she ever return . . . ?"

Marathons are very opening experiences. Right after one there is a tendency to feel naked, out of control. I sometimes feel slightly angry, but I have no reason for it. It is as though some big hole had been blasted in the belly of your self-defenses and suddenly you are standing naked as who you really are. After a marathon you try to make normal conversation with the other marathoners about the weather and how lovely it is to be a writer, but you feel as though you just lost your face. Don't worry, the state does pass and you become guarded and ornery again.

It is important to spend at least a half hour alone afterward. Doing something physical and concrete is helpful. Suddenly after a marathon I become an avid dishwasher or I madly plant twelve extra rows of bean plants where the grass seed was supposed to be planted. Just last week there was a marathon at my house, and before the last student left I had the vacuum cleaner out, vacuuming rugs in the living room where we had all just been sitting.

That naked feeling after a marathon is the same one I have felt often after a sesshin, a meditation retreat. After seven days of sitting meditation, we bow for the final time to Buddha and to the other Zen students, and then we usually have tea and cake treats in another room. After long periods of silence during the retreat, we can finally talk to each other. I always feel as though I want to smear the cake over my face so no one can see me. Once a close friend who visited with me on my porch right after a sesshin said, "You know, I feel like I'm sitting with a Cubist portrait of a woman by Picasso—all your dimensions are flashing at once!"

When I spend several hours alone writing, I have also felt this way. Do not worry about it. We are not used to being so open. It's fine, accept it; it is a good state to be in.

Claim Your Writing

Time and time again, I have experienced a peculiar phenomena in writing groups. Someone will write something extraordinary and then have no idea about its quality. It doesn't matter how much I may rave about it or the other people in the group give positive feedback; the writer cannot connect with the fact that it is good writing. He doesn't deny it; he just sits there bewildered and later, through the grapevine, I hear that he never believed a word of what was said. It's been over years that I have observed this; it isn't just one downtrodden, insecure character in one writing group that has not been awake to his own good writing.

We have trouble connecting with our own confident writing voice that is inside all of us, and even when we do connect and write well, we don't claim it. I am not saying that everyone is Shakespeare, but I am saying everyone has a genuine voice that can express his or her life with honest dignity and detail. There seems to be a gap between the greatness we are capable of and the way we see ourselves and, therefore, see our work.

The first time I became deeply aware of this was six years ago in a writing group I taught for eight weeks as a benefit for the Minnesota Zen Center. We all wrote about our family in simple, childlike terms—that was the assignment. We had fifteen minutes to write. There were twelve of us. When the time was up, we went around and each read what we had just written. I was the last one to read. The piece I read I later typed up and entitled "Slow Seeing the World Go Round," about my grandmother drinking water, raising children, and leaving the world without socks, salamis, or salt. After I read, there was silence for a long time.

Everything I say as a teacher is ultimately aimed at people trusting their own voice and writing from it. I try different angles and tricks. Once they do break through, all I teach is dressing on a turkey. The turkey is already roasting. I felt peaceful and happy; each student in the group had broken through resistance to a genuine, deeply felt piece of writing. There was nothing more I could say.

Suddenly, I looked around the room and everyone was watching me curiously, waiting to go on to another exercise. I was astounded. I realized none of them had any awareness of what they had just written. "None of you know that right now you wrote something very alive, do you?" They just kept looking at me.

This is not true only of beginning students. I am thinking now of two examples. One woman is a poet; she is very good and also very well loved. I call her the Darling of Minnesota. She writes about her life, her minister father, her seven sons, the breakfast table. At her last reading not only were all the seats filled, but they had sold out standing room. She told me that when the reading was over she went home very depressed because they had all liked her poetry so well. She said, "I fooled another crowd with my work."

The other example was a writer in one of my Sunday-night groups. She was a novelist and the assistant editor of a city magazine and had written two very successful plays; one was named Critics' Choice by the *Minneapolis Tribune*. She wrote several extraordinary pieces during timed writing in the group. I thought for sure she would know their quality—after all, she was an experienced writer. When I met her a month later for breakfast and commented about one of her pieces, she was amazed that I thought it was good. (*Good* wasn't the word for how good it was.) I was surprised that she herself didn't know. All her professional writing had been about subjects other than herself and her life's experiences. She said, "This kind of writing is all of you," so she couldn't see it.

Katagiri Roshi once said to me, "We are all Buddha. I can see you are Buddha. You don't believe me. When you see you are Buddha, you will be awake. That's what enlightenment is." It is very difficult for us to comprehend and value our own lives. It is much easier for us to see things outside ourselves. In the process of claiming our own good writing, we are chipping away at the blind gap between our own true nature and our conscious ability to see it. We learn to embrace ourselves as the fine creative human beings we are in the present. Occasionally, over time, we can see it: "Oh, I was good *then*," but it is in the past. We lag behind.

I do not mean for us all to become braggarts. I mean we should recognize that we are good inside and emanate our goodness and create something good outside us. That connection between our inner richness, our self-concept, and our work will give us a quiet peace and confidence that are hard for most artists to find. It is not "The work is bad and we are bad" or "The work is good and we are bad" or "The work is bad and we are good." It is "We are good and therefore we are capable of shining forth through our resistance to write well and claim it as our own." It is not as important for the world to claim it as it is to claim it for ourselves. That is the essential step. That will make us content. We are good, and when our work is good, it is good. We should acknowledge it and stand behind it.

Trust Yourself

In class Tuesday we went over two pages of someone's journal. The truth is it was my journal. Two pages of my journal. I selected them because I had pulled out a poem from those pages a few months ago. Not a great poem. A quiet poem. Those are tricky poems to find; they are the subtle hum in your notebook that can bring you into another world. I handed out copies of those two pages a week before. The students were to find the poem in them. They were also free to tell me if there was nothing there. "Nat, this is all junk."

Five or six students volunteered. There were at least four different versions of the poem. Some included the first half of the journal entry, some the middle, and one even picked up some overlapping work that was accidentally duplicated on the copy machine. There was one line they all included: "The hills of New Mexico are everywhere you go." All the versions sounded fine. None of them great poems, including the one I had chosen.

Give a piece to one hundred people, you could possibly get one hundred different opinions—not absolutely different, but lots of variations. This is where the depth of the relationship with yourself is so important. You should listen to what people say. Take in what they say. (Don't build a steel box around yourself.) Then make your own decision. It's your poem and your voice. There are no clear-cut rules; it is a relationship with yourself. What is it *you* wanted to say? What do you want to expose about yourself? Being naked in a piece is a loss of control. This is good. We're not in control anyway. People see you as you are. Sometimes we expose ourselves before we understand what we have done. That's hard, but even more painful is to freeze up and expose nothing. Plus freezing up makes for terrible writing.

The best test of a piece is over time. If you're not sure of something, put it away for a while. Look at it six months later. Things will be more clear. You might find that there are poems you love and that no one else cares about. I have one poem about a window that anyone who hears it uncategorically says is terrible. I think it's brilliant. When they ask me for my Nobel Prize speech, I'll whip out that little gem and have my satisfaction.

Don't worry if you come back six months later and the piece you weren't sure of turns out to be terrible. The good parts are already decomposing in your compost pile. Something good will come out. Have patience.

The Samurai

L AST NIGHT IN the Sunday-night group, I began
teaching about the Samurai part of writing and
ourselves. I realized that in class I have always been
very encouraging and positive. That was because we
were all in the creative space together. The encouragement was not dishonest; it naturally came out of
that noncritical, open field of creativity. Everything
you write is fine. And sometimes more than fine. It
absolutely burns through to shining first thoughts.
Sometimes students say, "Well, you're not being critical enough; I don't believe you." They don't realize
that we're sitting in different pools. I'm in the pool of
creativity; they are busy mixing up the creator and
editor and want to pull me into that fight. I don't
want to go there. It feels terrible.

But last night we started to work with the Samurai. Tom brought in a loosely finished piece, xeroxed
copies, and we went over it. First of all, we looked for
where there was energy. It was mainly in the third
paragraph. William Carlos Williams said to Allen
Ginsberg: "If only one line in the poem has energy,
then cut the rest out and leave only that one line."
That one line is the poem. Poetry is the carrier of life,

the vessel of vitality. Each line should be alive. Keep those parts of a piece; get rid of the rest.

The class played around with the third paragraph for a while. Not too long. Perhaps three minutes. That was enough. The third paragraph had energy but it wasn't hot. It wasn't half as hot as I knew Tom could be. I told Tom, "Yes, the third paragraph has energy. It's good to fiddle with it awhile. It might help to plant a seed for the future in your compost pile, but you'll come back to this one in a few weeks and it just doesn't quite burn through. We've spent enough time on it. Let's go on." Shirley (a newcomer to the group) interrupted, "Wait a minute. What's a Samurai?" Tom turned to her and spat out the answer: "Cut it out!"

So when you're in the Samurai space, you have to be tough. Not mean, but with the toughness of truth. And the truth is that the truth can never ultimately hurt. It makes the world clearer and the poems much more brilliant. I've been in writing workshops where we have worked on a bad poem, criticizing it for twenty minutes. That's ridiculous. It's a waste of time. It's like trying to beat a dead horse into running again. You can have the confidence that the writer of that poem will write other poems. You don't need to think that if you don't whip something out of the bad poem in front of you, the writer will never write again.

You can have the courage to be honest. "There's some good stuff in here, but it doesn't make it." And go on. It's a good process to be willing to just let go. Allen Ginsberg at Columbia University went up to his professor, the literary critic Mark Van Doren, and said, "How come you don't criticize work more?" His response was, "Why bother talking about something you don't like?"

During our writing there are times when we surface through the fog in our minds to some clarity—but not all the times that we become energetic in our writing mean that we have a valuable piece. No. They just mean we woke up, like on a Sunday morning after a late party Saturday night where we drank too much. Our eyes are open but we're not very alert. It's good to know where our writing is alive, awake, but it's where our writing is burning through to brilliance that it finally becomes a poem or prose piece. And anyone can hear the difference. Something that comes from the source, from first thoughts, wakes and energizes everyone. I've seen it many times in a writing group. When someone reads a really hot piece, it excites everyone.

Be willing to look at your work honestly. If something works, it works. If it doesn't, quit beating an old horse. Go on writing. Something else will come up. There's enough bad writing in the world. Write one good line, you'll be famous. Write a lot of lukewarm pieces, you'll put people to sleep.

Rereading and Rewriting

I T I S A good idea to wait awhile before you reread your writing. Time allows for distance and objectivity about your work. After you have filled a whole notebook in writing practice (perhaps it took you a month), sit down and reread the entire notebook as though it weren't yours. Become curious: "What did this person have to say?" Make yourself comfortable and settle down as though it were a good novel you were about to read. Read it page by page. Even if it seemed dull when you wrote it, now you will recognize its texture and rhythm.

When I reread my notebooks it never fails to remind me that I have a life, that I felt and thought and saw. It is very reaffirming, because sometimes writing seems useless and a waste of time. Suddenly you are sitting in your chair fascinated by your own mundane life. That's the great value of art—making the ordinary extraordinary. We awaken ourselves to the life we are living.

Another good value to rereading whole notebooks is that you can see how your mind works. Note where you could have pushed further and out of laziness or avoidance didn't. See where you are truly boring, how when you just complain in your writing it only leads you deeper into a pit. "I hate my life. I feel ugly. I wish I had more money. . . ." After you read your complaints long enough, you will learn to quickly turn to another subject when you are writing rather than linger too long in that complaint abyss.

Often while you are doing writing practice you have no idea whether you have written anything good or not. Sometimes I discover poems in my notebook that I did not know I had written. Our conscious minds are not always in control. On a day when I might have been subjectively bored while I was writing, it may turn out that I wrote a fine poem and didn't know it till a month later when I reread my work.

I remember once writing in my studio and feeling good with a sense of well-being. I kept saying to myself, "What are you so happy about? You haven't written anything good all day." Four days later I was teaching a journal class, and one of my students belligerently challenged me to prove that I, too, "write lots of junk" in my notebook. I thought, "What I wrote in the studio that day will be easy proof." I opened to that day's writing and began to read. To my amazement it was a moving piece about time passing and a roll call of all the people in my life who had passed on, either by moving away or by dying. My voice actually opened up as I read it. I was astounded.

That day in the studio my conscious mind was frustrated and had no idea that I had written anything good, but below my discursive, critical thoughts that buzz around like a swarm of mosquitoes, my hand was busy recording first thoughts and writing a very present piece. This can happen. Some part of us can walk through the cloud of humming mosquitoes and touch a very clear place inside us. We can ignore the negativity and constant chatter of the internal critic and continue to move our hand across the page. Our conscious minds are busy with the mosquitoes, so they aren't always aware that we are actually writing something good, but that day in the studio something was aware of it because I was humming the whole time. It is not unlike a mother who is constantly critical of her mothering, and yet you look at her children and see that they are happy, beautiful. She is doing a good job. Only in this case the mother (your discursive thoughts) and the good children (your writing) are both inside you and working simultaneously. The continuation of writing through all your discursive thoughts is the practice. A month later you recognize consciously the good writing when you reread your notebooks. At this point your unconscious and conscious selves meet, recognize each other, and become whole. This is art.

As you reread, circle whole sections that are good in your notebooks. They often glow off the page and are obvious. They can be used as beginning points for future writing, or they might be complete poems right there. Try typing them up. Seeing them in black and white makes it clear whether they work or not. Only take out the places where there is a blur, where your mind wasn't present. Don't change words, because in this practice you are deepening your ability to trust your own voice. If you were truly present when you wrote, it will be there whole. We don't need to now have our egos manipulate our words to sound better or the way we want to sound: perfect, happy, on top of everything. This is naked writing. It is an opportunity to view ourselves and reveal ourselves as we truly are and to simply accept ourselves without manipulation and aggression. "I am unhappy"—don't try to cover that statement up. Accept it without judgment if that's how you felt.

Naturally, there should be a place for editing and revision, but when we hear the word *editor,* we think, "Okay. I let the creator in me go wild, but now I'm going to get back to the proper, conventional, rational state of mind and finally get things in order." We bring out the man or woman in a tweed suit from the East Coast with a doctorate in literature who is critical of everything. Don't do that. That person in the tweed suit is just another disguise for the ego that is trying to get control of things any way it can. There should be no place in your writing for the ego to manipulate things the way it wants and to become picky. Instead, when you go over your work, become a Samurai, a great warrior with the courage to cut out anything that is not present. Like a Samurai with an empty mind who cuts his opponents in half, be willing to not be sentimental about your writing when you reread it. Look at it with a clear, piercing mind. But it is human nature to want to intrude and butt in with picky mind, so give your ego something to do. Let it type up your work, address the envelopes, lick the stamps. Just keep it out of your writing.

See revision as "envisioning again." If there are areas in your work where there is a blur or vagueness, you can simply see the picture again and add the details that will bring your work closer to your mind's picture. You can sit down and time yourself and add to the original work that second, third, or fourth time you wrote on something. For instance, you are writing about pastrami. Your first timed writing is good, but you know you have a lot more to say about the subject. Over a day, two days, a week's time, do several more timed writings on pastrami. Don't worry that you might repeat yourself. Reread them all and take the good parts of each one and combine them. It is like a cut-and-paste job, where you cut out the strong writings of each timed writing and paste them together.

So even in rewriting you use the method and rules of timed writing. This helps you to become reengaged in the work you wrote before. Attempting to reconnect with first thoughts is much better than standing in the middle of your mosquito swarm trying to swat at your discursive thoughts before they suck blood. It's a much more efficient way to rewrite, and it bypasses the ego even in rewriting. This method of rewriting can be used for short stories, essays, chapters of novels. A friend who just completed a novel said that when she had to rewrite a chapter she would say to herself, "Okay. This chapter needs these elements, and it has to begin in the grocery store and end in the cemetery. Go for an hour." The good parts from her timed rewritings of chapters were added to the original chapters to enrich and refine them.

Often you might read page after page in your notebooks and only come upon one, two, or three good lines. Don't be discouraged. Remember the football teams that practice many hours for a few games. Underline those good lines. Add them to your list of writing topics, and when you sit down to practice you can grab one of those lines and keep going. Underlining them also keeps you alert to them, and often you unconsciously use them. All these disparate parts suddenly come together, and you will be amazed.

I Don't Want to Die

S UZUKI ROSHI ESTABLISHED the San Francisco Zen Center and is the author of *Zen Mind, Beginner's Mind*. I have heard that he was a great Zen master. He died of cancer in 1971. When Zen masters die we like to think they will say something very inspiring as they are about to bite the Big Emptiness, something like "Hi-ho Silver!" or "Remember to wake up" or "Life is everlasting." Right before Suzuki Roshi's death, Katagiri Roshi, an old friend, visited him. Katagiri stood by the bedside; Suzuki looked up and said, "I don't want to die." That simple. He was who he was and said plainly what he felt in the moment. Katagiri bowed. "Thank you for your great effort."

Katagiri Roshi has said that when a spiritual person stands in front of a great art masterpiece, she feels peaceful. When an artist sees a masterpiece, it urges her on to create another one. An artist exudes vitality; a spiritual person exudes peace. But, says Katagiri, behind the peace of the spiritual person is tremendous liveliness and spontaneity, which is action in the moment. And an artist, though she expresses vitality, must behind it touch down on quiet peace; otherwise, the artist will burn out. Unfortunately, we have many examples of artists who have burned out through alcoholism, suicide, and mental illness.

So while we are busy writing, all the burning life we are eager to express should come out of a place of peace. This will help us and keep us from jumping around excitedly in the middle of a story and never quite getting back to our desk to finish it. Someplace in us should know the utter simplicity of saying what we feel—"I don't want to die"—at the moment of dying. Not in anger, self-recrimination, or self-pity, but out of an acceptance of the truth of who we are. If we can hit that level in our writing, we can touch down on something that will keep us going as writers. And though we would rather be in the high hills of Tibet than at our desks in Newark, New Jersey, and though death is howling at our backs and life is roaring at our faces, we can just begin to write, simply begin to write what we have to say.

EPILOGUE

I FINISHED TYPING Sunday night at eleven. I said to myself, "You know, Nat, I think the book is done." I stood up and was very angry. I felt used. ("Used by the muse," as my friend Miriam said later.) Suddenly I didn't know what the book was about; it didn't have anything to do with my life. It wouldn't find me a lover or brush my teeth in the morning. I took a bath, climbed out of the tub, dressed, walked alone at midnight to the Lone Wolfe Café in downtown Santa Fe. I ordered a glass of white wine and two scoops of toffee ice cream. I looked at everyone, spoke to no one, and kept smiling: "I've finished a book. Soon maybe I can be a human being again." I walked home relieved and happy. The next morning I cried. By the afternoon I felt wonderful.

On Tuesday I told my writing class: "The book took a year and a half to write. At least half of the chapters came out whole the first time. The biggest struggle was not with the actual writing, but working out the fear of success, the fear of failure, and finally burning through to just pure activity." The last month and a half I wrote seven days a week. I finished one chapter and began another. That simple. The parts of me that were screaming for Häagen Dazs ice cream, for friends, for daydreaming, I did not listen to.

Anything we fully do is an alone journey. No matter how happy your friends may be for you, how much they support you, you can't expect anyone to match the intensity of your emotions or to completely understand what you went through. This is not sour grapes. You are alone when you write a book. Accept that and take in any love and support that is given to you, but don't have expectations of how it is supposed to be.

This is important to know. We have an idea that success is a happy occasion. Success can also be lonely, isolating, disappointing. It makes sense that it is everything. Give yourself the space to feel whatever you feel, and don't feel as though you shouldn't have a wide range of emotions. Katagiri Roshi once told me, "That's very nice if they want to publish you, but don't pay too much attention to it. It will toss you away. Just continue to write." Two days ago I told my father, "I'm going to jump off the Empire State Building." He said, "Do you have to pick such a high building?" I tell myself, "Natalie, this book is done. You will write another one."

AFTERWORD

An Interview with the Author

Q: Do you think there's a connection between place and the inspiration to write?

I think land and environment are very important. Often, for instance in a novel, place is the third character. It's palpable in really good novels. But I don't think you have to be in a gorgeous place to write. I don't think you have to be in your heart's song. I think you just have to be where you are. In other words, if you're in Cincinnati, if you can really eat Cincinnati, know the streets and the weather, the trees, how the light looks at the end of your workday, that's what's important. Now, for me, I had a great love for Taos. It was almost a lover. And it was actually painful because I couldn't always be there. And, especially at the beginning, I couldn't make a living there. And yet Taos was my passion. But once I got to live there full-time, as I do now, then I remembered Katagiri Roshi, my Zen teacher, saying, "Even paradise gets stinky," and he was right. When you know a place well, it's a place. You might love it deeply, but it's a place that has good and bad things. But having this place gives you a freedom to go anyplace and appreciate and love other places. Which wasn't true for me before, because I was always fighting where I was, because I wanted to be in Taos.

Don't do that to yourself—"I am here, but I should be there." It was torture for me. Wherever you are is the place to be writing from. Don't use the excuse that you are not in the right place. There is no perfect place. Just pick up your pen, record the details of where you are. Writing will show you that you are in the perfect place right now. Land is the earth. Earth is your life, moment by moment.

Q: What are the "I can't write because" excuses that you hear the most?

People offer me thousands of excuses about why they can't write. "I'm afraid to let myself out." "I'm afraid to follow what I really want." "I can't do it now but it's my deepest dream." "I can't do it now because I have a family." "I have to make a living." "I am scared that I'm not good enough." "I'm afraid my father will kill me if I write about him." I don't pay attention at that level. All I see is that they are using some excuse, that they want something and they are not stepping forward and taking hold of it. Over the years what I've watched is that people don't let themselves burn. They don't let their passion be alive and then feed it. But I don't listen to their excuses. After a while it's boring. Just like my complaining is boring.

It's monkey mind. It doesn't really matter what the excuse is. I can hear you saying, "Well, but isn't it true? What if they do have six children and they need to feed them and they need a job?" Absolutely. But if they burn to write, they also have to find time to write, even if it's one-half hour a week. They can't put it off till they're sixty. They might die at fifty-nine. You have to somehow address your whole life. We can't put things off. Now, you could say, "Well, Natalie, you don't have children. You don't have this. You don't have that." It's not about that. I remember being in a group where a woman was saying, "Oh, I feel so lonely"; you know, "I have so many kids and I have a husband and I'm so busy but I still feel lonely." And I said, "That's odd. I don't have any of that and I feel lonely." I think it's the human predicament. We give a lot of names to our excuses, to the reasons we don't want to write or we're afraid to. Finally, if you want to write, you have to just shut up, pick up a pen, and do it. I'm sorry there are no true excuses. This is our life. Step forward. Maybe it's only for ten minutes. That's okay. To write feels better than all the excuses.

I had a group of students a few years ago who'd studied with me many times. I went around the room and said to them, "Well, what do you need now?" And they started in: "Well, you know, I haven't been writing because my wife is such and such and my life is such and such." I looked at them and said, "You know what to do, pick up a pen and write." And their faces lit up and they said, "Oh, okay." And I said, "Wait a minute. You traveled all the way from Chicago, from Boston, Kentucky, L.A., you've taken three other seminars with me. You already know this." They said, "Yeah, but we needed to hear it again." I was aghast. I said, "You came all the way here just to hear it?" They said yes. Something so simple and obvious, but we keep missing it. We need to discover it over and over. I remember this particular person I'm thinking of, his face was just glowing after I said it again, because he had thought this time it wouldn't work, that this time there was really a problem big enough— and he was believing it—that it was so solid he could not write. He was so relieved to come back to this direct phrase: shut up and write. We have tremendously strong monkey minds that are very creative and always thinking of new reasons why we can't write. Don't believe your excuses.

Q: What is monkey mind?

Monkey mind is actually a Buddhist term. We could also call monkey mind the editor or the critic. Something that creates busyness to keep us away from our true heart. Our whole culture is built on busyness. And that's why we're so unhappy. But we love busyness. We have to understand it. There's busyness, there's monkey mind, and then there's our true heart. What does our true heart want? We have to give it at least 50 percent. Otherwise we fill our whole life with busyness. I have to do this, I'm going here, I'm making that. Daily life is very seductive. Weeks go by and we forget who we are.

Q: What about talent?

I think talent is like a water table under the earth—you tap it with your effort and it comes through you. I see many students who come to me who can naturally write beautifully. You can't believe it—the first time they pick up a pen, the rest of my students' mouths hang open. But sometimes it's too easy for them, so these people don't believe that what they wrote was good. Sometimes it just doesn't mean that much to them. But someone I see sitting in the corner of the room, who struggles the whole time, who seems a little nerdy, a little bland—ah, but three years later the person is still showing up. After a while, this writer's little coal is beginning to glow. That's wonderful.

I never thought of myself as talented. No one ever told me I had any talent. Anytime I went to a palm reader, an astrologer, I was told I should be an accountant. So it was my effort, my determination, that made new lines in my palm. I guess I've always believed in human effort. Human effort is not just the hard physical work of putting your shoulder to the grindstone. What I'm talking about is work that wakes us up. We all have that ability within us. Talent has nothing to do with waking up. I'm talking about being aware and mindful as a writer. Knowing the names of trees and plants, noticing the sun and how it's hitting the chrome on a car. That comes with practice. It's pretty nice to be talented. If you are, enjoy, but it won't take you that far. Work takes you a lot further.

Q: How is writing affected by Zen practice?

Writing has always been connected with my Zen practice and with mindfulness and meditation. Art for art's sake never interested me, because I've seen many unhappy artists whose egos are very much solidified. In this case the practice of art engenders suffering. But if you know you have nothingness at your back, emptiness, you can't crystallize as easily. For me, writing is always connected with that kind of emptiness. You can create a word because there was no word there before. There was a blank page. If everything was filled, there'd be nothing you could step into. So I guess art, creativity, without meditation practice doesn't interest me. Zen has always been at my back.

Q: What about benefiting others with your writing?

I don't think that much of self-expression. I am definitely writing to benefit other people. But it's tricky because I don't want to please other people. I want to be able to say the truth, but I don't say it for myself anymore. I think when I was a poet I wrote a lot of stories. There was definitely some self-expression in there and my need to feel that I could say anything. I used a lot of four-letter words in my poems, kind of stick-my-tongue-out-at-everybody—see, I can do whatever I want. Now I'm much more interested in communicating. How do I communicate through language, black words on a white page, to other people all over the country, so that I can hopefully hand some of my clarity, when I have it, to someone else? So I don't care that much about self-expression anymore, though that might be a good beginning, a way to learn to assert yourself. Now when I'm writing and all of me is doing it, I'm out of the way, not a hindrance. Writing does writing. Instead of self-expression, it's a wonderful letting go of Natalie Goldberg. I get to go beyond myself. I think if I were just doing self-expression, I could sit down and fill a journal and say, "I'm so happy today, I fell in love, I love my boyfriend so much, he's so cute," and someone else would read it and be bored. To learn to communicate beyond ourselves we have to let go of our immediate expression and go deeper, honor the significance of details, touch things as they are.

Q: What is the difference between meditation and writing practice?

When I'm sitting, the object is to let go of thoughts and anchor my mind with my breath in the present moment. But, of course, it's not so easy. When you sit a lot, you see that those thoughts are sticky and they keep coming back. In writing practice, you grab these thoughts and write them down, and by writing them down, you go on to the next one and you keep moving through them. You are anchoring your mind with your pen. Your thoughts become a quick stream you're sitting in. So they're not quite as sticky. In a sense, writing practice is a more expedient way of settling into a quiet place. I get to run through the thoughts and then let them go; whereas when I sit, there's no place to spit them out and they take a long time to digest. They just hang around, roll around in the mouth of my mind. So it's a different process. It's a parallel process. Writing is my deepest Zen practice.

The most important thing I've learned through sitting and writing is that thoughts are not real, they're not solid. That we pay too much attention to them. That there's tremendous freedom in letting go of them. But that's easier said than done, because thoughts connect with emotions and you hook up a story and a past and memories, and in three minutes you're psychotic. But if you can catch them at the root, at the simple level of the thought first arising, it's very helpful. For instance, I'll have an argument with my lover and I'll believe in my point of view. Then sometimes grace comes along and I'll hear this little voice in me say, "Nat, it's just your position, it doesn't really mean anything, let it go." And wow, does that create space.

Whatever is in front of you is your life, so please

take care of it. I don't sit in the zendo trying to think what to write and then run to my notebook and try to capture what I thought. Each place is a different experience. Playing music is a step removed from the moment in the zendo, but it's not a step removed from actually blowing that clarinet. That's that moment. Painting—when I'm painting—it's not a step removed. And when I'm writing, it's not a step removed. They are just different mediums with which to meet yourself and the world. Watching your breath, being present with your whole body, is the medium of the zendo. Words are the medium of writing. When your words are alive, they are electric beings—they are not one jot removed or distant from human life. When I'm brushing my teeth, I'm afraid I daydream a lot, but sometimes I'm there brushing my teeth.

Q: Tell us a little about writing a novel.

A novel doesn't work the way the mind moves. The way I wrote *Writing Down the Bones* was natural to the way the mind moves. When I wrote the novel *Banana Rose,* I had to have something in chapter 3, like a brown hat, have meaning in chapter 33. Now, in our life a brown hat might not always have much meaning. Your car breaks down, it might just be that the car broke down. We have many thoughts. They come and go. No great meaning. But in a novel we have this tremendous need to tell a story, create meaning. So there has to be a structure, a beginning, a middle, and an end, even if it's not obvious. The reader's mind yearns for meaning. So I had to learn the structure of a novel, which was different from the natural movement of the mind that I'd been studying all along and that writing practice is based on. It was very hard for me. Because of that, I don't think I'm naturally a novelist. I don't look for meaning. A novelist would say, "I'm not looking for meaning either." But things have to fit together. In the end, when you finish reading a novel, you have to feel "ah." And if it doesn't work, there's no "ah," no settling into a certain rightness or a completeness inside you.

Once I began writing the novel, I was committed. I was willing to do whatever I had to to make the novel work. I never knew I had that kind of effort in me. I would sit at the Harwood Library in Taos and rework things and rework them again. The summer went by. I watched it go through the high windows at the library. And then I saw fall come. I felt as though I were in fourth grade: I'd been left back; everybody else had a summer vacation and I had to finish some composition. I couldn't believe my determination. I'll never forget that. That's the awe I feel. It might not be the greatest novel, but it was my greatest effort. And that effort is actually what gives me—I don't know if you call it confidence—but my own spine. I really did it the best Natalie could have ever done it at that point in her life, and I'm proud of it. I'll always love Nell, the main character.

You know, maybe *that* is my talent. Tremendous determination. In this one area: writing. Not in other areas. For instance, I run around the block once— uh, I don't want to do it anymore. I stop. Skiing: I fell, oh, I don't like skiing; I take off my skis. But in writing I have that determination.

Q: Why do you write memoir?

I like it. Memoir is a study of how memory works. It's analogous to writing practice, to working with the mind. Memory doesn't remember chronologically A, B, C. I was born in such-and-such a year, I went to this public school, then I did this, then I did that. We remember in flashes. You see a glint off a fork. Boom, you suddenly remember the hot dog you ate at Coney Island twenty years ago. It works in slices. And I love that. And when you write memoir, its structure is more analogous to the way the mind moves than a novel's is. And I love stories, family stories, where people come from, all kinds of things like that. I was in New York and I met this terrific Zen teacher. She's quite large and jolly and has a shaved head. Well, we were talking, and it came out that her mother was a beauty queen and she had seven stepfathers. I went wild. Here she is, a strict Zen person, you'd never in a zillion years guess her background. I loved the juxtaposition. I couldn't stop asking her questions. It's important for people to spend some time digging into their past in their writing practice because there should be no place that you're avoiding. If you avoid it in yourself, you're going to avoid it whatever you write about, and that pollutes the writing. You need to be able to stand up with your life. Accept your mind and your life.

Q: How did writing practice come about?

I discovered this relationship with my mind. I was sitting a lot of zazen in Taos when I was a hippie, and I went up to Colorado in 1976 to study with Allen Ginsberg for six weeks at Naropa Institute in Boulder. He taught the examination of thoughts and writing. And I continued it. I feel as though he was the visionary and I was the worker bee that documented it. He said, "When the mind is shapely, your writing will be shapely." I did a little retreat by myself before I went to Naropa, and I found an article in the retreat house that he had written in which he talks about polishing the mind. I didn't understand all of it, but it piqued my interest, and I made a promise to myself that someday I would understand it all. Nobody I'd ever heard talked about the mind when I studied literature in college and grad school.

I started to write and time myself and keep my hand moving. I explored the vast space of what was possible on the page—where my mind traveled, backward, forward, upside down. I had no goal, no product direction. I watched how I thought. I came into some kind of intimate relationship with myself. I was alone. I wasn't sure what I was doing, but it was so compelling that I went deeper and deeper into it. I noticed things: how repetitious the mind can be, how to dive below discursive thinking, how to use the details in front of me to ground myself. I didn't call it monkey mind then, but I was meeting it. I saw that certain things helped me write and other things didn't help me write. This timed practice gave me a structure; I wasn't going to go crazy. Whatever came up, I kept my hand moving, and I stayed there until the time was up. Just as in meditation, whatever comes up while you're meditating, you keep the structure of the posture until the bell rings.

When I met Katagiri Roshi, he said, "Make writing your practice" at a time when I never listened to anything he said. I was arrogant. So I said, "Oh, that's ridiculous, Roshi." And I didn't pay attention to it because writing seemed antithetical to Zen practice at that time. I thought he was just trying to get rid of me. You know, "Get out of here, Natalie, we don't want you in the zendo." I said, "No, I'm going to keep sitting." But over the years I began to refine my understanding of my writing. I knew I had grasped something powerful and was riding its wild back. Eventually, over many years, I called it writing practice. I began to understand what Katagiri had told me. It was actually in the writing of *Writing Down the Bones* that it all came together, that a great "ah" occurred. About two years after the book was out, I went to see Roshi. I asked him, "Why did you tell me to make writing my practice?" He looked at me very nonchalantly and said, "Well, you like to write. That's why I told you." I said, "You mean that simple?" He said, "You just like to do it." So way back then he understood where my passion was. If you really want to be a runner but you think you should meditate, make running your practice and go deeply into it at all levels. But he also said it's pretty good to sit too. So my heart was into writing, but I also sat to keep myself honest. And to somehow develop my back, my spine. You know, my front was all energy. You have to have quiet peace at your back. Otherwise you burn up.

Q: What if someone is afraid of losing control?

To be alive, we have to deal with a loss of control. Falling in love is a loss of control. When we die or someone we love dies, it's a tremendous loss of control. And what's nice about writing practice is it's a measured way to dip yourself into that huge vast emptiness, that loss of control, and then pull yourself out so you can feel safe again. You put down your pen for a while and go take a walk. Then you dip yourself in. Sort of in degrees. That's really what the East gave to the West. When they gave us meditation practice, they gave us a structure to go into the emptiness of the mind without going berserk. So for anyone who is afraid of losing control: Write with other people. Don't worry, there are people around you. And we'll support you. And we're all in the same boat. Keep your hand moving. Don't worry.

Q: How do I choose the right topic for a book?

It has to come from a deep place, and it's not an idea or "topic," like a school composition. It's a longing that comes from the bottom of the well. For instance, my body is preparing to write a book that I probably will start soon, but it's been years in the making. I wasn't aware of it, but I have been living it. When it dawned on me that I wanted to write about it, for six months it composted in my belly, and I know that soon I'll start it. I'll sit down and say, "Go," but you have to make sure that a book comes from a deep passion or even obsession. Because a book takes a long time to write, and you can't burn out after you've written only ten pages. And it's not good to start a book and then quit, because you'll build up a pattern. I know many people who start books and never finish them. So it's good to sit with it for a while and let it burn deep. Do a lot of writing practice around it. Make sure you really care enough. Because I'll tell you, when you start writing a book, you go under for a long time.

Q: What would you say to Natalie when she was working on Writing Down the Bones?

I couldn't tell her anything. She was who she was. She wouldn't hear me. For instance, one of the things I'd say now is you don't realize that getting well-known and being successful can be pretty hard and pretty painful. I could say that. I say that to my students. They don't want to hear it. They want what they want. Natalie at thirty-six years old wanted to burn through. I don't know why, but I wanted to be famous. I think I unconsciously thought it would save my life. Of course, it didn't save my life. But I couldn't tell her any of that. I just look back and I feel tremendous love and compassion for her. She was so earnest. She worked so hard. And she was so innocent. And in some ways she was smarter, she hadn't been broken as much, and I think we see certain kinds of things more clearly when we're not as broken. There's nothing in the way. We don't have fear. Of course, we don't know what the consequences and results will be. The results will come when they come.

Writing this book was particularly powerful because for the first time I had to say what I thought, saw, and felt. And I had to stand up behind it with no encouragement. It was my first book. No one but me cared if I wrote it. After you write one book and it's successful, you feel a little more confident that even though people might think you're an idiot, they'll listen—at least for a moment. I'd been put down a lot in my life and I wasn't cheered on as a kid. And so I had to stand up behind this book. It was very scary. I had to say the way I saw things. And I didn't know if people would think I was crazy. There's a skin or membrane in society that you have to pierce, and you pierce it with your effort. I had to get behind myself, break through, and finally I was listened to.

Q: How did you develop that kind of confidence?

I have tremendous confidence and trust in my own mind. Now what does that mean? That I'll be brilliant? No. Most people are smarter and much more talented then I am. I'm not putting myself down. When I say, "I trust what I say," I mean that I give it value and I listen to it. I believe in the integrity of my mind. And the other thing that has given me great confidence is that if I say I'm going to write three hours today, I will write for three hours. Now that seems very simple, what's the big deal? But in other areas of my life—for instance, I'll say I'll stop eating chocolate, but I don't stop. I have no confidence in myself there. But in writing I have confidence. Because I say I'm going to do it and I do it. That's all. Writing is the one thing in my life I continually show up for. I have given 100 percent to writing practice. That's what builds confidence.

But with my Zen practice, I think it's a little different, not as muscular, determined, forceful. I have a quiet noodle way in Zen practice. But I do keep in

there. You don't have to be a bulldog or a shot out
of a cannon. Just noodle your way in. Find your way
as a noodle. That noodle way might be smarter as a
writer, too.

Q: How do you build this confidence in your students?
I am their cheerleader. Go, go, go, you can do it.
When I step into that role as a teacher, I see their
greatness. I don't pay attention to all of their "I can't
do it because of this or that." I pay no attention to it.
I see all of their greatness. I care about the whole
health of a writing life, how we continue. Not just
one magnificent jab.

Q: What does "Don't be tossed away" mean?
Don't be tossed away by your monkey mind. You
say you want to do something—"I really want to be a
writer"—then that little voice comes along, "but I
might not make enough money as a writer." "Oh,
okay, then I won't write." That's being tossed away.
These little voices are constantly going to be nagging
us. If you make a decision to do something, you do it.
Don't be tossed away. But part of not being tossed
away is understanding your mind, not believing it so
much when it comes up with all these objections and
then loads you with all these insecurities and reasons
not to do something.

As I got closer to finishing this book, I had tremendous fear both of failure and of success. I stopped

working on *Bones* for almost six months and became a baker at a restaurant on Canyon Road in Santa Fe. One day during a break I took a walk by the acequia, and I fell down sobbing, and I said, "Nat, you have to do it for Katagiri, forget about yourself." And that gave me the drive to do it. In my mind I grabbed on to Katagiri and told myself, "I'm doing it for him." I have as much insecurity as anybody else, but I don't pay attention to myself so much when I'm in the process of doing something that I really want. I don't think, "Natalie, do you want it? Don't you want it?" Because that fear of success and failure stops me. If I think of myself, I get caught in myself, like everyone else. First my insecurities, then my overblown idea of myself. I swing from one extreme to the other. But if I forget myself, then I can do it. Don't be thrown off by yourself or anyone else. Let your big mind move forward.

At the time I was writing this book, I felt this tremendous love for Katagiri Roshi. When I say love, I mean beyond anything I'd ever felt. And maybe I needed to share that with readers. But that great love was something bigger than good or bad. He had pulled true Natalie out of me. So, big Natalie wanted to do it for big Katagiri. And now what I understand is that big Natalie and big Katagiri were never separate. But that's not psychological. That's the truth. It was my idea that I was less than him or different from him. Even many years later, long after his death,

I was tortured. You know, I lost the great being of my life. He died. The great freedom for me came when I understood that we were never separate and that I was him and he was me. That huge love helped me not to be tossed away. In completing this book, I felt a willingness to step up to the plate. It was my time to stop clinging to myself, to take deeper vows. To take on this writing life, and practice was for me to realize that I was capable of what Katagiri Roshi was capable of.

This afterword is adapted from an interview with Tami Simon of Sounds True. Used with permission.

NOTES

1. William Carlos Williams, "Detail," in *The Collected Earlier Poems* (New York: New Directions, 1938).

2. Ernest Hemingway, *A Moveable Feast* (New York: Charles Scribner's Sons, 1964).

3. Cesar Vallejo, "Black Stone Lying on a White Stone," in *Neruda and Vallejo,* ed. Robert Bly (Boston: Beacon Press, 1971).

4. Williams, "The Red Wheelbarrow," in *The Collected Earlier Poems.*

5. Marisha Chamberlain, ed., *Shout, Applaud* (St. Paul, Minn.: COMPAS, 1976).

6. Russell Edson, *With Sincerest Regrets* (Providence, R.I.: Burning Deck, 1980). Reprinted with permission of the publisher.

7. Williams, "Daisy," in *The Collected Earlier Poems.*

8. William Blake, "The Auguries of Innocence," in *The Norton Anthology of Poetry* (New York: W. W. Norton, 1970).

9. Interview with Allen Ginsberg and Robert Duncan, in *Allen Verbatim,* ed. Gordon Ball (New York: McGraw-Hill, 1974).

10. Both from Carolyn Forché, "Dawn on the Harpeth," unpublished poem given to the author. Printed with permission.

11. Richard Hugo, "Time to Remember Sangster," in *What Thou Lovest Well, Remains American* (New York: W. W. Norton, 1975).

12. Richard Hugo, "Why I Think of Dumar Sadly," in *What Thou Lovest Well, Remains American*.

13. From Kate Green, "Journal: July 16, 1981," in *If the World Is Running Out* (Duluth, Minn.: Holy Cow! Press, 1983). Reprinted by permission of the author and the publisher.

14. From Anne Sexton, "Angel of Beach Houses and Picnics," in *The Book of Folly* (Boston: Houghton Mifflin, 1972).

15. Poems by Shiki and Issa from *Haiku: Eastern Culture*, vol. 1, trans. R. H. Blyth (Tokyo: Hokuseido Press, 1981). Poems by Basho and Buson from *Haiku: Spring*, vol. 2, trans. R. H. Blyth (Tokyo: Hokuseido Press, 1981).

BOOKS AND AUDIO BY NATALIE GOLDBERG

Books

Chicken and in Love
Wild Mind: Living the Writer's Life
Long Quiet Highway: Waking Up in America
Banana Rose: A Novel
*Thunder and Lightning: Cracking Open the
    Writer's Craft*
Top of My Lungs: Poems and Paintings
Living Color: A Writer Paints Her World
The Essential Writer's Notebook
The Great Failure: My Unexpected Path to Truth
Old Friend from Far Away: How to Write Memoir

For more information, visit www.nataliegoldberg.com.

Audio Resources from Sounds True

Writing Down the Bones
The best-selling guide to writing as a spiritual practice, read in its entirety, with additional commentary and an interview.

7 CDs / 8 ¾ hours / $44.95 / Order #W409D

The Writing Life: Ideas and Inspiration for Anyone Who Wants to Write

An instructive conversation between Julia Cameron (author of *The Artist's Way*) and Natalie Goldberg on the writer's craft.

      2 CDs / 2 1/2 hours / $19.95 / Order #w443D

Long Quiet Highway: A Memoir on Zen in America and the Writing Life

A heartfelt memoir, read aloud and including an interview unavailable elsewhere.

Digital download only / 8 1/2 hours / $48.97 / Order #w403W

Old Friend from Far Away: How to Write Memoir

Learn to write vivid, naturally structured memoirs using Goldberg's favorite exercises for connecting with the senses and making memory vibrant.

      2 CDs / 2 1/2 hours / $24.95 / Order #w598D

Zen Howl: Revealing This One Great Life

Goldberg joins a Zen teacher to explore the surprisingly close connection between writing and Zen, and how this understanding can strengthen both practices.

      2 CDs / 2 1/2 hours / $24.95 / Order #w683D

The Great Failure: My Unexpected Path to Truth

A candid exploration of Natalie Goldberg's life, making sense of primary relationships between father and daughter, teacher and student. Read in its entirety, concluding with an exclusive Sounds True interview.

6 CDs / 6 3/4 hours / $29.95 / Order #W873D

To order any of these programs, call Sounds True toll-free at 1-800-333-9185, or visit their website, *www.soundstrue.com*. Many of these programs are also available as digital downloads from the Sounds True website.

CREDITS